PENGUIN BOOKS

PATRICK WHITE SPEAKS

Patrick White was born in England in 1912, when his parents were in Europe for two years; at six months he was taken back to Australia, where his father owned a sheep station. At the age of thirteen he was sent to school in England, to Cheltenham, 'where, it was understood, the climate would be temperate and a colonial acceptable'. Neither proved true, and after four rather miserable years there he went to King's College, Cambridge, where he specialized in languages. After leaving the university he settled in London, determined to become a writer. His first novel, *Happy Valley*, was published in 1939 and his second, *The Living and the Dead*, in 1941. During the war he was an RAF Intelligence Officer in the Middle East and Greece. After the war he returned to Australia.

His other novels are *The Aunt's Story* (1946), *The Tree of Man* (1956), *Voss* (1957), *Riders in the Chariot* (1961), *The Solid Mandala* (1966), *The Vivisector* (1970), *The Eye of the Storm* (1973), *A Fringe of Leaves* (1976) and *The Twyborn Affair* (1979). In addition he published two collections of short stories, *The Burnt Ones* (1964) and *The Cockatoos* (1974), which incorporates several short novels, the collection of novellas *Three Uneasy Pieces* (1987) and his autobiography, *Flaws in the Glass* (1981). He also edited *Memoirs of Many in One* (1986). In 1973 he was awarded the Nobel Prize for Literature.

Patrick White died in September 1990. In a tribute to him *The Times* wrote, 'Patrick White did more than any other writer to put Australian literature on the international map ... his tormented *oeuvre* is that of a great and essentially modern writer.'

PATRICK WHITE SPEAKS

PENGUIN BOOKS

PENGUIN BOOKS

Published by the Penguin Group
Penguin Books Ltd, 27 Wrights Lane, London W8 5TZ, England
Penguin Books USA Inc., 375 Hudson Street, New York, New York 10014, USA
Penguin Books Australia Ltd, Ringwood, Victoria, Australia
Penguin Books Canada Ltd, 10 Alcorn Avenue, Toronto, Ontario, Canada M4V 3B2
Penguin Books (NZ) Ltd, 182–190 Wairau Road, Auckland 10, New Zealand

Penguin Books Ltd, Registered Offices: Harmondsworth, Middlesex, England

First published in Great Britain by Jonathan Cape 1990
Published in Penguin Books 1992
10 9 8 7 6 5 4 3 2 1

Printed in England by Clays Ltd, St Ives plc

Contents

Contents

Editors' Note

We would like to thank the following people and organisations: Patrick White for his original typescripts where available; Barbara Mobbs, literary agent, for her gentle husbandry; David Marr for his free-trading in sources and suggestions — his biography of Patrick White will be published by Random/Cape; Craig McGregor for permission to use his Patrick White monologue from *In the Making* (Nelson, Melbourne, 1969) which he co-edited with David Beal, David Moore and Harry Williamson; Paul Murphy and the Australian Broadcasting Commission for permission to use his *Nationwide* interview (ABC-TV 17 March 1981); Penny Coleing for her early speech collecting; Janet Hawley for quotes from her interview; Joe Beaumont for 'the usual'; Jeff Carter for photo tips; and Alf Liebhold for his suggestions and photographic assistance. Thanks also to Desirée Flynn, Alban Gillezeau, Luc Lucas and Amanda Vogel for proof-reading and suggestions; and to the many people who tried hard to remember or were helpful in other ways including Eve Abbey, Ron Abbey, Wendy Bacon, Faith Bandler, Meredith Burgmann, Marian Hill, Nance Loney, Hugh Mason, Jack Mundey, Neil Runcie, and Dulcie Stretton.

Further acknowledgements for texts to: *Australian Letters* for 'The Prodigal Son'; *Wildlife and the Environment* for 'A Living Living-Room'; *Builder's Labourer* for 'Civilization, Money and Concrete'; Imprimerie Royale P.A. Norstedt & Soner for 'The Nobel Prize'; *Abbey's Broadsheet* for 'Australian of the Year'; *Meanjin Quarterly* for 'Tribute to the Whitlam Government'; *Grenfell Record* for 'Australian of the Year'; *Courier Mail* for 'We Must Not Turn Back ...'; *Australian Library News* for 'Wide and Independent Reading is What Matters'; ABC Radio archives for 'Farewell to Whitlam'; National Book Council for 'The Awards Dinner'; *AICD Factsheet* for 'Speech Delivered by Patrick White'; Croom Helm Australia for *Australia and Nuclear War* ed. by Michael Denborough; *Sydney Morning Herald* for 'It Seems As Though Life Itself ...'; *Arena* for 'In this World of Hypocrisy and Cynicism ...'; ABC Enterprises for *Imagining the Real* eds Dorothy Green & David Headon; *Blast* for 'The Bicentenary'; and *Overland* for 'Credo'.

We regret that despite much ferretting, no-one involved in the occasion of Patrick White's launching of Manning Clarke's *History of Australia: Volume Four 1851-1888* in March 1978, was able to find the text of that speech.

Acknowledgements and special thanks for photographs to: Roslyn Poignant for Axel Poignant's portraits (photos 1 & 2); to David Moore for his garden portrait (photo 4); and to Barry O. Jones (MP) for his bicentennial photo (photo 23). Thanks also to Lindsay Howe, Reprography Section, La Trobe University; and Lee McDonald, Features Bureau, John Fairfax & Sons. Acknowledgements also to Peter Moxam/SMH 1974 (photo 10); Kevin Berry/SMH 1976 (photo 12) *and* (photo 13); Julian Zakaras/SMH 1982 (photo 15); Bruce Miller/SMH 1986 (photo 21); John Fairfax & Sons; News Ltd.; *Canberra Times; Herald & Weekly Times*. While every effort has been made to trace and acknowledge photograph copyright holders, the publishers tender their apologies for any unintended infringement where the copyright holder has proved untraceable.

Asterisks (*) in text indicate *Note* at the end of the book.

Paul Brennan
Christine Flynn

PATRICK WHITE'S parents, a pastoralist family from the Upper Hunter region in New South Wales, were in London when he was born in 1912. They brought him back to Australia as a six months old baby. At thirteen he was sent off to England for secondary schooling. At eighteen he persuaded his parents to let him return to Australia to work as a jackeroo before being sent back to England again to study at Cambridge University. White's first novel *Happy Valley* was published in London in 1939 and *The Living and the Dead* in 1941. In 1940 White was commissioned as an Air Force intelligence officer and served in the Middle East. During this time he met Manoly Lascaris, 'who has remained the mainstay of my life and work'. They returned to live in Australia in 1948. *The Aunt's Story* was published that year; *The Tree of Man* in 1955 and *Voss* in 1957.

In 1958 White wrote this article for the journal *Australian Letters*. The journal introduced him as 'perhaps Australia's greatest living novelist'. Other than an occasional letter to a newspaper, it was White's first foray into public debate.

The Prodigal Son

1958

THIS IS by way of being an answer to Alister Kershaw's recent article *The Last Expatriate,* but as I cannot hope to equal the slash and dash of Kershaw's journalistic weapons, I shall not attempt to answer him point by point. In any case, the reasons why anybody is an expatriate, or why another chooses to return home, are such personal ones that the question can only be answered in a personal way.

At the age of 46 I have spent just on twenty of those years overseas. During the last ten, I have hardly stirred from the six acres of 'Dogwoods', Castle Hill. It sounds odd, and is perhaps worth trying to explain.

Brought up to believe in the maxim: Only the British can be right, I did accept this during the earlier part of my life. Ironed out in an English public school and finished off at King's, Cambridge, it was not until 1939, after wandering by myself through most of Western Europe, and finally most of the United States, that I began to grow up and think my own thoughts. The War did the rest. What had seemed a brilliant, intellectual, highly desirable existence, became distressingly parasitic and pointless. There is nothing like a rain of bombs to start one trying to assess one's own achievement. Sitting at night in his London bed-sitting room during the first months of the Blitz, this chromium-plated Australian with two fairly successful novels to his credit came to the conclusion that his achievement was practically nil. Perhaps significantly, he was reading at that time Eyre's *Journal.* Perhaps also he had the wind up; certainly he reached rather often for the bottle

13

of Calvados in the wardrobe. Any way, he experienced those first sensations of rootlessness which Alister Kershaw has deplored and explained as the 'desire to nuzzle once more at the benevolent teats of the mother country'.

All through the War in the Middle East there persisted a longing to return to the scenes of childhood, which is, after all, the purest well from which the creative artist draws. Aggravated further by the terrible nostalgia of the desert landscapes, this desire was almost quenched by the year I spent stationed in Greece, where perfection presents itself on every hand, not only the perfection of antiquity, but that of nature, and the warmth of human relationships expressed in daily living. Why didn't I stay in Greece? I was tempted to. Perhaps it was the realisation that even the most genuine resident Hellenophile accepts automatically the vaguely comic role of Levantine beachcomber. He does not belong, the natives seem to say, not without affection; it is sad for him, but he is nothing. While the Hellenophile continues humbly to hope.

So I did not stay in my elective Greece. Demobilisation in England left me with the alternative of remaining in what I then felt to be an actual and spiritual graveyard, with the prospect of ceasing to be an artist and turning instead into that most sterile of beings, a London intellectual, or of returning home, to the stimulus of time remembered. Quite honestly, the thought of a full belly influenced me as well, after toying with the soft, sweet awfulness of horsemeat stew in the London restaurants that I could afford. So I came home. I bought a farm at Castle Hill, and with a Greek friend and partner, Manoly Lascaris, started to grow flowers and vegetables, and to breed Schnauzers and Saanen goats.

The first years I was content with these activities, and to soak myself in landscape. If anybody mentioned Writing, I would reply: 'Oh, one day, perhaps'. But I had no real intention of giving the matter sufficient thought. *The Aunt's Story,* written immediately after the War, before returning to Australia, had succeeded with overseas critics, failed as usual with the local ones, remained half-read, it was obvious from the state of the pages in the lending libraries. Nothing seemed important, beyond living and eating, with a roof of one's own over one's head.

Then, suddenly, I began to grow discontented. Perhaps, in spite of Australian critics, writing novels was the only thing I could do with any degree of success; even my half-failures were some justification of an otherwise meaningless life. Returning sentimentally to a country I had left in my youth, what had I really found? Was there anything to prevent me packing my bag and leaving like Alister Kershaw and so many other artists? Bitterly I had to admit, no. In all directions stretched the Great Australian Emptiness, in which the mind is the least of possessions, in which the rich man is the important man, in which the schoolmaster and the journalist rule what intellectual roost there is, in which beautiful youths and girls stare at life through blind blue eyes, in which human teeth fall like autumn leaves, the buttocks of cars grow hourly glassier, food means cake and steak, muscles prevail, and the march of material ugliness does not raise a quiver from the average nerves.

It was the exaltation of the 'average' that made me panic most, and in this frame of mind, in spite of myself, I began to conceive another novel. Because the void I had to fill was so immense, I wanted to try to suggest in this book every possible aspect of life, through the lives of an ordinary man and woman. But at the same time I wanted to discover the extraordinary behind the ordinary, the mystery and the poetry which alone could make bearable the lives of such people, and incidentally, my own life since my return.

So I began to write *The Tree of Man.* How it was received by the more important Australian critics is now ancient history. Afterwards I wrote *Voss,* possibly conceived during the early days of the Blitz, when I sat reading Eyre's *Journal* in a London bed-sitting room. Nourished by months spent trapesing backwards and forwards across the Egyptian and Cyrenaican deserts, influenced by the arch-megalomaniac of the day, the idea finally matured after reading contemporary accounts of Leichhardt's expeditions and A. H. Chisholm's *Strange New World* on returning to Australia.

It would be irrelevant to discuss here the literary aspects of the novel. More important are those intentions of the author which have pleased some readers without their knowing exactly why, and helped to increase the rage of those who have found the book meaningless. Always something of a frustrated painter, and a composer *manqué*, I wanted to give my book the textures of music, the sensuousness of paint, to convey through the theme and characters of *Voss* what Delacroix and Blake might have seen, what Mahler and Liszt might have heard. Above all I was determined to prove that the Australian novel is not necessarily the dreary, dun-coloured offspring of journalistic realism. On the whole, the world has been convinced, only here, at the present moment, the dingoes are howling unmercifully.

What, then, have been the rewards of this returned expatriate? I remember when, in the flush of success after my first novel, an old and wise Australian journalist called Guy Innes came to interview me in my London flat. He asked me whether I wanted to go back. I had just 'arrived'; who was I to want to go back? 'Ah, but when you do,' he persisted, 'the colours will come flooding back onto your palette.' This gentle criticism of my first novel only occurred to me as such in recent years. But I think perhaps Guy Innes has been right.

So, amongst the rewards, there is refreshed landscape which even in its shabbier, remembered version has always made a background to my life. The worlds of plants and music may never have revealed themselves had I sat talking brilliantly to Alister Kershaw over a Pernod on the Left Bank. Possibly all art flowers more readily in silence. Certainly the state of simplicity and humility is the only desirable one for artist or for man. While to reach it may be impossible, to attempt to do so is imperative. Stripped of almost everything that I had considered desirable and necessary, I began to try. Writing, which had meant the practice of an art by a polished mind in civilised surroundings, became a struggle to create completely fresh forms out of the rocks and sticks of words. I began to see things for the first time. Even the boredom and frustration presented avenues for endless exploration; even the ugliness, the bags and iron of Australian life, acquired a meaning. As for the cat's cradle of human intercourse, this was necessarily simplified, often bungled, sometimes touching. Its very tentativeness can be reward. There is always the possibility that the book lent, the record played, may lead to communication between human beings. There is the possibility that one may be helping to people a barely inhabited country with a race possessed of understanding.

These, then, are some of the reasons why an expatriate has stayed, in the face of those disappointments which follow inevitably upon his return. Abstract and unconvincing, the Alister Kershaws will probably answer, but such reasons, as I have already suggested, are a personal matter. More concrete, and most rewarding of all, are the many letters I have received from unknown Australians, for whom my writing seems to have opened a window. To me, the letters alone are reason enough for staying.

IN THE early 1960s White's first four plays, *Ham Funeral, Season at Sarsaparilla, A Cheery Soul* and *Night on Bald Mountain* were performed. By the end of the 1960s he had three more books written and published — *Riders in the Chariot* (1961), a collection of stories *The Burnt Ones* (1964), and *The Solid Mandala* (1966).

The year before the publication of *The Vivisector* (1970), Craig McGregor spent many hours talking with Patrick White. From these talks McGregor created the following monologue, published in a book he co-edited called *In the Making*.

In the Making

1969

RELIGION. Yes, that's behind all my books. What I am interested in is the relationship between the blundering human being and God. I belong to no church, but I have a religious faith; it's an attempt to express that, among other things, that I try to do. Whether he confesses to being religious or not, everyone has a religious faith of a kind. I myself am a blundering human being with a belief in God who made us and we got out of hand, a kind of Frankenstein monster. Everyone can make mistakes, including God. I believe God does intervene; I think there is a Divine Power, a Creator, who has an influence on human beings if they are willing to be open to him. Yes, I pray. I was brought up an Anglican. Oh, then I gave that away completely. After the war I tried to belong to the Church of England, but I found that so completely unsatisfactory. I wouldn't say I am a Christian; I can't aspire so high. I am a very low form of human being; in my next incarnation I shall probably turn up as a dog or a stone. I can't divorce Christianity from other religions. The Jewish, for instance, is a wonderful religion — I had to investigate it very thoroughly for *Riders in the Chariot*. In my books I have lifted bits from various religions in trying to come to a better understanding; I've made use of religious themes and symbols. Now, as the world becomes more pagan, one has to lead people in the same direction in a different way ...

I'm really more interested in things urban than things country, in the more sophisticated aspects of Australian life ... though I come from the country, it's in my blood. The novel I am working on now is set mainly in Sydney. It's about the life of a painter, I've known many painters myself. One of the first I knew was Roy de Maistre: I feel he taught me to write by teaching me to look at paintings and get beneath the surface. I've seen a lot of Nolan on and off, he's a friend of mine; and Lawrence Daws, Rapotec. I like some of Fred Williams's paintings very much; I think he gets closer to the essence of the Australian landscape than most. Why can't a writer use writing as a painter uses paint? I try to. When I wrote *The Tree of Man* I felt I couldn't write about simple, illiterate people in a perfectly literate way; but in my present novel the language is more sophisticated. I think perhaps I have clarified my style quite a lot over the years. I find it a great help to hear the language going on around me; not that what I write, the narrative, is idiomatic Australian, but the whole work has a balance and rhythm which is influenced by what is going on around you. When you first write the narrative it might be unconscious, but when you come to work it over you do it more consciously. It gives what I am writing a greater feeling of reality. When I came back from overseas I felt I had to learn the language again. That is one of the reasons I work in Australia. I write about Australia; you have to do a certain amount of research; and I think it's a good thing to be close to one's roots. It's a good thing, too, to spend some time away from them; it enriches your work, Martin Boyd, Christina Stead — *Cotter's England*, that's a terrific novel. They went away and stayed away. The essence of what you have to say you pick up before you're twenty, really, so it ought to be possible to go away and draw on that. I came back. I work better here because there are no distractions. It would be so boring if I didn't write I would go mad…

I have been working on this present novel for three years. Oh, and I've written the first draft of a novella as well. I always like to write three versions of a book. The first is always agony and chaos; no one could understand it. With the second you get the shape, it's more or less all right. I write both of those in longhand. The third draft I type out with two fingers: it's for refining of meaning, additions and subtractions. I think

my novels usually begin with characters; you have them floating about in your head and it may be years before they get
together in a situation. Characters interest me more than situations. I don't think any of my books have what you call plots.
I used to take notes, once upon a time; and sometimes I begin
with a very slight skeleton. But I always think of my novels
as being the lives of the characters. They are largely something that rises up out of my unconscious; I draw very little
on actual people, though one does put a bow or a frill on from
here or there. I find the actual bits, if you do use them, are
most unconvincing compared to the fictitious bits. Sometimes
characters do enlarge as you write, but within the rough
framework of what you had intended. It's fatal to hurry into
a book; the book I like least, *The Living and the Dead*, I had
to hurry because of the war. *The Tree of Man* took me four
years. I rewrite endlessly, sentence by sentence; it's more like
oxywelding than writing. Once I used to write at night, from
midnight till four o'clock in the morning; but as I got older
I decided that was a strain, so now I get up at five and write
through the morning and then perhaps from five to seven in
the evening. The afternoon is death for anything; I sleep. I
have the same idea with all my books: an attempt to come
close to the core of reality, the structure of reality, as opposed
to the merely superficial. The realistic novel is remote from
art. A novel should heighten life, should give one an illuminating experience; it shouldn't set out what you know already.
I just muddle away at it. One gets flashes here and there,
which help. I am not a philosopher or an intellectual. Practically anything I have done of any worth I feel I have done
through my intuition, not my mind — which the intellectuals
disapprove of. And that is why I am anathema to certain kinds
of Australian intellectual. It irritates me when I think of some
of those academic turds, and the great Panjandrum of Canberra who described my writing as pretentious and illiterate
verbal sludge...One can't tell in one's own lifetime if what
one has written is any good; I feel what I've written is better
than some other people's. I like *The Aunt's Story* and *The Solid
Mandala* best — the first because for so long nobody would

pay any attention to it, and even those who did take any notice didn't read it — I went into Angus & Robertson's library, just twenty-five years ago, and noticed that people had read only the first quarter, they were the only pages which were soiled; and *The Solid Mandala* because it's a very personal kind of book, I suppose, and comes closest to what I've wanted.

I've lost interest in the theatre because you can't get what you want ever. I used to think it would be wonderful to see what you had written come to life. Here in Australia it's very hard to get an adequate performance because of the state of the theatre; but even if you have the best actors in the world it's never what you visualised. One can't say all one wants to say, one can't convey it. Chekov is one of the exceptions who had the kind of subtlety I would like to get into the theatre. I've always been stage-struck. I wanted to become an actor when I was young, but fortunately I became too self-conscious at the English public school I went to. I think it's better to be a writer than an actor. Acting is a very untidy kind of life, it's all very ephemeral; your novel might last, but your performance won't. And I'm not really interested in happenings and all that kind of rubbish. Not so long ago I thought of writing an opera; I had this idea that I thought would have made a good opera. But it didn't work out. A waste of time, really. I'd better keep on writing novels. Short stories? I don't really like writing them so much — though I have nearly got enough for another volume. All my effects are cumulative, and one doesn't really have the time to get the effects you want. The novella is more satisfactory; you can put more into it. Sometimes if I become very depressed while writing a novel and I get an idea for a short story I get that down, and afterwards I feel as though I have been liberated somehow.

I am not writing for an audience; I am writing, and if I have an audience I am very glad. I shocked some people the other night by saying writing is really like shitting; and then, reading the letters of Pushkin a little later, I found he said exactly the same thing! It's something you have to get out of you. I didn't write for a long time at one stage, and built up such an accumulation of shit that I wrote *The Tree of Man*. I wouldn't call myself a humanist; I am indifferent to people in general. But I have always been gregarious. This myth that I'm not has been put about by bitches that I wouldn't have in my house. I like people, but I like to choose my people. I'm not isolated; I know quite a lot of people in the theatre, in the art world. When we first came back to Australia we lived at Castle Hill because we wanted to live in the bush, and yet be close to the city. Then it became just another suburb; we were surrounded by little boxes. So we moved closer in. It makes it easier to have people to dinner, go to the theatre, films. Harry Miller took an option on *Voss* to make it into a film, but we could never agree on a director.

Which writers have influenced me? Joyce and Lawrence, certainly. Lawrence I liked so much in my youth I'd be afraid to read him now. The nineteenth century Russians, too. Then at Cambridge I did a degree in French and German literature, so I got to know something about that. Proust influenced everybody. I seem to do less and less reading, especially fiction, though I reread *Madame Bovary* not so long ago when I was having a pause from writing — it really knocked me right over, it was so wonderful. When I was in Dublin I reread Joyce's *Dubliners* and realised I'd missed out on half of it before. Of the American novelists the people I like are Bellow and Updike, who are fairly detached. They owe their quality to their detachment.

I am interested in detail. I enjoy decoration. By accumulating this mass of detail you throw light on things in a longer sense: in the long run it all adds up. It creates a texture — how shall I put it — a background, a period, which makes everything you write that much more convincing. Of course, all artists are terrible egoists. Unconsciously you are largely writing about yourself. I could never write anything factual; I only have confidence in myself when I am another character. All the characters in my books are myself, but they are a kind of disguise.

Nine Thoughts from Sydney

1970

1

To sublimate an incestuous passion for an aunt,
Mr Antrobus has let lantana overrun his garden:
Cats prowl and scream at dusk;
Everywhere this stench of cat pee.

2

All the bullock waggoners are dead,
The horse teams stuck for ever,
Manes beaded with Paddo mud:
This is Harry Miller's Day.

3

The hot nights have perhaps discouraged burglars.
As ladies knotting their own hair
Hope to be entered brutally
A sound of clocks, not sandshoes, overcomes.

4

First the abos, then the Irish,
Now it's the Hungarians,
Witchetties kosher-killed and paprikashed;
But the same old ghosts rise to haunt towers in
                                    lavatory brick.

5

My telescope trained on
Every one of the fifty-seven windows,
Witnesses only potplants
And an imitation Francis Bacon.

6

Where is the politician who will flower like the
                              leptospermum citrata,
Who will sound like the surf out of the Antarctic,
Who has in his hands the knots of coolibah,
And in his soul the tears of migrants landing
                              from Piraeus?

7

I will not travel nights by off-peak buses:
Neither smoke nor her can-opening laugh
Encourages the freckled conductress to believe
Her penis ever stood.

8

Mrs de Tintacks in her tiny Bondi shack
(a Dobell in the dunny, Sculthorpe piped above the sink)
Watches her Poseidons rise.
Seed pearls grate beneath her eyelids as
She reaches out and turns the butler on.

9

Whereas the Australian metal was iron,
Brass is brighter, flash and brash.
Beware the trumpet that blows too loud:
Its echoes are *Saturday Evening Post.*

———•••———

APROPOSAL by the New South Wales Government to take over sections of Centennial and Moore Parks, part of Australia's oldest parkland, for an Olympic sports complex provoked protests. White's house was one of those to be demolished to make way for the complex. At a family picnic rally in the Park on Sunday, 18 June he stepped into the political arena as a speaker for the first time. He had just turned sixty. He threatened to leave Australia if the complex was built. 'No snail', he said, 'likes to have his house crushed. Unlike the snail I can build another. But, like the snail, part of me would be left behind.'

A Living Living-Room

1972

Coming down here not so long ago to collect signatures for the petition to help save the parks — from what, we all by now know all about, I met a man who told me, 'It's time you conservationists got into step with progress'. I didn't start an argument about 'progress', because that is one of the mystic words nobody seems able to define. I simply asked, 'Do you want the park to die, then?' He replied, 'So what? It's only a park.' It gave me a slight shiver, as I think all you who are here today — who know and use this park — will understand. It is obvious by now that there are thousands of people in this city who are not exclusively obsessed by bashing a ball or panting around a track — people who, in an over-organised life, look forward to moments of personal freedom when they can become relaxed human beings. There is no reason why those who are dedicated to sport should not enjoy it, in some more appropriate part of Sydney, certainly not three miles from its business centre, and by the ruin of a park which compares with the most beautiful in the world. For me, personally, these are Hyde Park, London and the Pincio, Rome. These of course had a start of centuries over Centennial Park. That they have endured for centuries is because generations have respected them as a delight to the eye and for many other homely, more down-to-earth reasons. As I understand it, a park is certainly not a Luna Park, with a music bowl, public address system, cycle tracks, traffic whizzing along raised roadways, and a great concrete amphitheatre looming over it, with a crowd roaring monotonously inside. As *you* know, you who use and appreciate this park, it's a place where you can sit in natural surroundings and eat a picnic lunch with the kids, feed any stale bread to the ducks, escape from your box after a dingdong — after that same dingdong, make it up, nowhere more agreeably. A park is a living living-room, in which to do anything and nothing — rest your fallen arches, or roam through the wilder parts exercising your imagination, or simply breathing — most important the breathing. And it will become increasingly important as this reckless anti-civilisation gathers momentum. Your parks are your breathing spaces. Guard them, cherish them. I'm speaking particularly of the younger ones among you, because, if we win this battle, as I'm sure we shall, even in a world where the worst very often happens, there will be other attempts during your lifetime to steal or spoil your parks. Parkland is valuable, and greedy eyes see the money in it. So you must always be on the alert. Hang on to your breathing spaces in this developing and already over-congested city. Protect your parks from the pressure of political concrete.

HAVING spoken to the people in Centennial Park that morning, White led a march through the city streets to Sydney Town Hall and spoke again.

Over the next few years he became an active environmentalist, giving his support to groups and individuals opposing the mining of uranium and rutile sand. In 1975 he became a founder of the Friends of the Green Bans Movement together with Jack Mundey (Builders Labourers' Federation), Charles Birch (Professor of Biology) and Geoff Mosley (Director Australian Conservation Foundation). The Green Bans were refusals by unions to work on developments which would cause the destruction of historical sites.

Mad Hatter's Party

1972

I MUST have stood in this Town Hall for the first time in 1917. I would have been five years old. I was brought here to a fancy dress ball, dressed as the Mad Hatter from *Alice in Wonderland*. Sometimes in 1972 — held up, say, at the Edgecliff lights, waiting to plunge on towards the city, where so much has been torn down you can look through practically as far as this Town Hall — I feel there is still some kind of Mad Hatter's party going on — in the name of progress. What, I wonder, constitutes this progress we are urged to believe in? Perhaps the vision of some American city of the 1930s when for most other countries of the world the United States was the symbol of material success. But what of today? As our well-travelled politicians are driven round Manhattan or Chicago are none of them aware of the neuroses and despair, the dirt and violence lurking in these ever-crowded concrete warrens? If our travelled politicians are not aware, many thinking Americans would be prepared to give warning. In fact, some of these thinking Americans have migrated to Australia, to escape from what we now seem to be building up for ourselves in imitation of America. Take the city of Sydney — this sports complex: a great concrete growth which the Minister for Lands proposes to plant only three miles from the city's heart. Just stop to think of the effect this ganglion will have on the traffic of an already congested metropolis, on the nerves of those struggling to reach their homes after a sporting event, to say nothing of the nerves of anyone who lives in its vicinity. Nor does this take into account the loss of breathing space by the absorption of one park, and encroachment on a second which is one of the radiant features of our city. It seems incredible that those acting for our good have not given more thought to the doubtful blessing they are wishing on us, when there are other sites in the sprawl of Sydney far more suited, and where in fact there is a demand for some focus point of interest as this sports complex would give the deprived inhabitants. Take, for instance, a recently developed suburb such as Fairfield. A few years ago this was goat country; I used to take my own goats to the buck at Fairfield-Smithfield. But with the influx of migrants, this district has become comparatively populous. I have a friend who goes there talking to the schools. She tells me that hardly any of the children, their parents still working overtime to establish themselves in their new country — scarcely any of these children have been even as far as the city, seen the harbour, visited the zoo. Television is the only stimulus they have in their lives. For all I know there are other growing suburbs like Fairfield whose need for a diversion like this sports complex is not only reasonable and humane, it is their right. Before it is too late, let us consider these unused tracts of land at Homebush as probably the logical site for such an important sports complex and possible expo ground of the future. That part of Sydney will soon become, we must realise, the population centre of this great city. The Government itself, which wants to plonk a sports complex on what in one sense amounts to a perimeter, has shown it recognises the drift of population outward. What about the plan to move Sydney Hospital to Parramatta? This plan was shelved, and rightly: the hospital must continue to serve the army of workers employed by day in the city proper. But the Government has gone ahead, wisely, with the plan to build a big new hospital at Westmead to serve this other area of increasing population. If logic works in one field, surely it can in another? Or do our business interests blinker us to the truth? In closing, I'm going to hark back to that same fancy dress ball to which I was brought in 1917. I can remember a young woman wearing nothing but a few sheets of newspaper round her middle and a pair of high-heeled shoes. She represented *The Naked Truth*. Today the truth is a good deal nakeder than she was. If, paradoxically, she is even more elusive, that does not mean we must ever relax in our truthful pursuit of her.

RESIDENTS of the inner Sydney suburb of Kings Cross and their supporters, in a long and contentious campaign, got organised to fight evictions and stop high rise development which would have destroyed heritage houses in Victoria Street. White addressed one of their meetings held in the Wayside Chapel in August. It was tense. Bullies who supported the developers were hanging around.

Civilisation, Money and Concrete

1973

W<small>HAT SEEMS</small> to me to be overlooked continually by those who plan building development is the reaction of the ones who are most closely affected by the development — the human beings who are to be disposed of like sheep or cattle. I had this brought home to me when the street where I live was suddenly threatened with demolition. So in this respect I can sympathise personally with the inhabitants of Victoria Street. It becomes a more personal matter when to think of growing up only a stone's throw from here in Roslyn Gardens, I seemed to spend more of my early life trudging these streets on errands of one kind or another. So that in a sense I, too, am part of this neighbourhood — spiritually part of it, I like to think. Only recently politicians have come to recognise the rights of Aborigines to their tribal lands — not only as traditional hunting grounds, but because they are filled with associations of the spirit. When, I wonder, will politicians, and aldermen in particular, recognise that white Australians too have a right to their tribal lands? Some residents of Victoria Street have in some cases, I understand, lived all their lives in houses where their parents lived before them. What is to become of such people is one of the great problems in this developing city. They can't be merely evicted — even brutally evicted as there is evidence in this neighbourhood. I feel that such communities must be actively encouraged to continue in pockets throughout the city, assisted if necessary to improve their houses — not to turn them into unnatural show places, but to preserve quiet streets here and there, as necessary for everybody's well-being as those other breath-ing spaces, our periodically threatened parks.

Half the trouble in the development business — and local government for that matter — seems to me to arise from the fact that there are developers and aldermen who have no deep-rooted connexion with the cities they are developing and governing. Coming from remote countries, they are not truly conscious of the spirit of place. A stadium or another sky-scraper plonked down where it suits them and their business allies is only another stepping stone on their road to spec-tacular material success. To be perfectly frank they are out to pluck the innocent goose, becoming over-night millionaires as well as Knights of the Askin Round Table*. If we imply that these men are foreigners, we must also own up to their Australian counterpart our own wizards of the quick dollar, as well as give thanks for the thousands of foreign migrants who have made Australian life more interesting, fruitful, and efficient in the last few decades — helping us towards what we haven't yet got, but which we may achieve in time — a civilisation. Let us aim at this rather than what they refer to as 'progress', a materialistic, and what may turn out to be a meaningless term. Civilisation is not a matter of money and concrete. (Look at what's become of the United States!) Civil-isation, as I see it, depends on spirit — human beings — human values.

PATRICK WHITE was told he had won the 1973 Nobel Prize for Literature on the night of 18 October. *The Eye of the Storm* had been released in September and particularly impressed members of the Royal Swedish Academy of Letters. With their house besieged by journalists, Manoly Lascaris predicted, 'our lives will never be the same'. White consented to interviews on his verandah the following morning, and to pose for photographers the whole day.

He did not go to Stockholm to accept the prize because it would have been dangerous with his chronic asthma to travel from a Sydney summer to a Scandinavian winter. Instead he asked friend Sidney Nolan, living in London, to accept the prize on his behalf from the King of Sweden on 10 December. Nolan obliged.

By way of official recognition, Prime Minister Gough Whitlam invited White to the House of Representatives to formally receive national congratulations. White declined. 'This is the kind of situation', he replied, 'to which my nature does not easily adapt itself'.

White used his $80,000 prize to set up The Patrick White Literary Award for older writers who have not received the recognition they deserve. He donated his prize medal and diploma to the State Library of New South Wales, rather than 'leave them in a drawer waiting for burglars'.

This is the autobiographical essay originally published in Sweden in association with the Nobel Prize.

The Nobel Prize

1973

I WAS BORN on 28 May 1912 in Knightsbridge, London, to Australian parents. Victor White was then forty-two, his wife Ruth Withycombe ten years younger. When I was six months old my parents returned to Australia and settled in Sydney, principally because my mother could not face the prospect of too many sisters-in-law on the property in which my father had an interest with three older brothers. Both my father's and my mother's family were yeoman-farmer stock from Somerset, England. My Great-Grandfather White had emigrated to New South Wales in 1826, as a flockmaster, and received a grant of Crown land in the Upper Hunter Valley. None of my ancestors was distinguished enough to be remembered, though there is a pleasing legend that a Withycombe was a fool to Edward II. My Withycombe grandfather emigrated later in the Nineteenth Century. After his marriage with an Australian, he and my grandmother sailed for England, but returned when my mother was a year old. Grandfather Withycombe seems to have found difficulty in settling: he drifted from one property to another, finally dying near Muswellbrook on the Upper Hunter. My father and mother were second cousins, though they did not meet till shortly before their marriage. The Withycombes enjoyed less material success than the Whites, which perhaps accounted for my mother's sense of her own superiority in White circles. Almost all the Whites remained wedded to the land, and there was something peculiar, even shocking, about any member of the family who left it. To become any kind of artist would have been unthinkable. Like everybody else I was intended for the land, though vaguely I knew this was not to be.

My childhood was a sickly one. It was found that I was suffering from nothing worse than asthma, but even so, nobody would insure my life. As a result of the asthma I was sent to school in the country, and only visited Sydney for brief, violently asthmatic sojourns on my way to a house we owned in the Blue Mountains. Probably induced by the asthma I started reading and writing early on, my literary efforts from the age of about nine running chiefly to poetry and plays. When thirteen I was uprooted from Australia and put at school at Cheltenham, England, as my mother was of the opinion that what is English is best, and my father, though a chauvinistic Australian, respected most of her caprices. After seeing me 'settled' in my English prison, my parents and sister left for Australia. In spite of holidays when I was free to visit London theatres and explore the countryside, I spent four very miserable years as a colonial at an English school. My parents returned for the long holidays when I was sixteen, and there were travels in Europe, including Scandinavia. Norway and Sweden made a particular impression on me as I had discovered Ibsen and Strindberg in my early teens — a taste my English housemaster deplored: 'you have a morbid kink I mean to stamp out': and he then proceeded to stamp it deeper in.

When I was rising eighteen I persuaded my parents to let me return to Australia and at least see whether I could adapt myself to life on the land before going up to Cambridge. For two years I worked as jackeroo, first in the mountainous southern New South Wales, which became for me the bleakest place on earth, then on the property of a Withycombe uncle in the flat, blistering north, plagued alternately by drought and flood, I can remember swimming my horse through flood-waters to fetch the mail, and enjoying a dish of stewed nettles during a dearth of vegetables. The life in itself was not uncongenial, but the talk was endlessly of wool and weather. I developed the habit of writing novels behind a closed door, or at my uncle's, on the dining table. More reprehensible still, after being a colonial at my English school, I was now a 'Pom' in the ears of my fellow countrymen. I hardly dared open my mouth, and welcomed the opportunity of escaping to King's College, Cambridge. Even if a university should turn out to be another version of a school. I had decided I could lose myself afterwards as an anonymous particle of the London I already loved.

In fact I enjoyed every minute of my life at King's, especially the discovery of French and German literature. Each vacation I visited either France or Germany to improve my languages. I wrote fitfully, bad plays, worse poetry. Then, after taking my degree, the decision had to be made: what to do? It was embarrassing to announce that I meant to stay in London and become a writer when I had next to nothing to show. To my surprise my bewildered father, who read little beyond newspapers and stud-books, and to whom I could never say a word if we found ourselves stranded alone in a room, agreed to let me have a small allowance on which to live while trying to write.

At this period of my life I was in love with the theatre and was in and out of it three or four nights of the week, I tried unsuccessfully to get work behind the scenes. I continued writing the bad plays which fortunately nobody would produce, just as no one did me the unkindness of publishing my early novels. A few sketches and lyrics appeared in topical revues, a few poems were printed in literary magazines. Then, early in 1939, a novel I had managed to finish, called *Happy Valley*, was published in London, due to the fact that Geoffrey Grigson the poet, then editor of the magazine *New Verse* which had accepted one of my poems, was also reader for a publishing firm. This novel, although derivative and in many ways inconsiderable, was well enough received by the critics to make me feel I had become a writer. I left for New York expecting to repeat my success, only to be turned down by almost every publisher in that city, till the Viking Press, my American publishers of a lifetime, thought of taking me on.

This exhilarating personal situation was somewhat spoilt by the outbreak of war. During the early, comparatively uneventful months I hovered between London and New York writing too hurriedly a second novel *The Living and the Dead*. In 1940 I was commissioned as an air force intelligence officer in spite of complete ignorance of what I was supposed to do. After a few hair-raising weeks amongst the RAF great at Fighter Command I was sent zig-zagging from Greenland to the Azores in a Liverpool cargo boat with a gaggle of equally raw intelligence officers, till finally we landed on the Gold Coast, to be flown by exotic stages to Cairo, in an aeroplane out of Jules Verne.

The part I played in the War was a pretty insignificant one. My work as an operational intelligence officer was at most useful. Much of the time was spent advancing or retreating across deserts, sitting waiting in dust-ridden tents, or again in that other desert, a headquarters. At least I saw something of almost every country in the Middle East. Occasionally during those years bombs or gunfire created what should have been a reality, but which in fact made reality seem more remote. I was unable to write, and this finally became the explanation of my state of mind: my flawed self has only ever felt intensely alive in the fictions I create.

Perhaps the most important moments of my war were when, in the Western Desert of Egypt, I conceived the idea of one day writing a novel about a megalomaniac German, probably an explorer in Nineteenth Century Australia, and when I met the Greek friend Manoly Lascaris who has remained the mainstay of my life and work.

After demobilisation we decided to come to Australia where we bought a farm at Castle Hill outside Sydney. During the war I had thought with longing of the Australian landscape. This and the graveyard of post-war London, and the ignoble desire to fill my belly, drove me to burn my European bridges. In the meantime, in London, in Alexandria on the way out, and on the decks of liners, I was writing *The Aunt's Story*. It was exhilarating to be free to express myself again, but nobody engaged in sorting themselves out of the rubble left by a world war could take much interest in novels. Australians, who were less involved, were also less concerned. Most of them found the book unreadable. Just as our speech was unintelligible during those first years at Castle Hill, I had never felt such a foreigner. The failure of *The Aunt's Story* and the need to learn a language afresh made me wonder whether I should ever write another word. Our efforts at farming — growing fruit, vegetables, flowers, breeding dogs and goats, were amateurish, but consuming. The hollow in which we lived, or perhaps the pollen from the paspalum which was always threatening to engulf us, or the suspicion that my life had taken a wrong turning, encouraged the worst attacks of asthma I had so far experienced. In the eighteen years we spent at Castle Hill, enslaved more than anything by the trees we had planted, I was in and out of hospitals. Then about 1951 I began writing again, painfully, a novel I called in the beginning *A Life Sentence on Earth*, but which developed into *The Tree of Man*. Well received in England and the United States, it was greeted with cries of scorn and incredulity in Australia: that somebody, at best a dubious Australian, should flout the naturalistic tradition, or worse, that a member of the grazier class should aspire to a calling which was the prerogative of school-teachers! *Voss*, which followed, fared no better: it was 'mystical, ambiguous, obscure': a newspaper printed its review under the headline *Australia's Most Unreadable Novelist*. In *Riders in the Chariot* it was the scene in which Himmelfarb the Jewish refugee is subjected to a mock crucifixion by drunken workmates which outraged the blokes and the bluestockings alike. Naturally, 'it couldn't happen here' — except that it does, in all quarters, in many infinitely humiliating ways, as I, a foreigner in my own country, learned from personal experience.

A number of Australians, however, discovered they were able to read a reprint of *The Aunt's Story*, a book which had baffled them when first published after the War, and by the time *The Solid Mandala* appeared, it was realised I might be something they had to put up with.

In 1964, submerged by the suburbs reaching farther into the country, we left Castle Hill, and moved into the centre of the city. Looking back, I must also have had an unconscious desire to bring my life full circle by returning to the scenes of my childhood, as well as the conscious wish to extend my range by writing about more sophisticated Australians, as I have done in *The Vivisector* and *The Eye of the Storm*. On the edge of Centennial Park, an idyllic landscape surrounded by a metropolis, I have had the best of both worlds. I have tried to celebrate the park, which means so much to so many of us, in *The Eye of the Storm* and in some of the shorter novels of *The Cockatoos*. Here I hope to continue living, and while I still have the strength, to people the Australian emptiness in the only way I am able.

FIVE HUNDRED VIP diners sat in Melbourne Town Hall on 25 January watching Patrick White accept his wooden plaque as Australian of the Year 1973. He had been unanimously chosen by the judges. Some of those chosen before him had been Shane Gould (swimmer), Evonne Goolagong (tennis player), Cardinal Gilroy and Lord Casey (Governor General).

A few weeks later White wrote to the Federal Government calling for an official protest against the arrest of fellow Nobel Prize winner, the Soviet writer Alexander Solzhenitsyn. Solzhenitsyn had been arrested following his objection to turning himself in to the KGB for 'voluntary questioning'.

White's second collection of stories, *The Cockatoos*, came out the same year.

Australian of the Year

1974

PERHAPS I should preface my few words by saying I was born a pessimist. This at least means that when the best very occasionally happens it comes as an agreeable surprise. After that I must out and say (to the disgust of many Australians) that Australia Day is for me a day of self-searching rather than trumpet-blowing. We in this Lucky Country * are inveterate trumpet-blowers and what I fear for us is that, if we don't take care, we shall end up in the late Twentieth Century as kid brother of the original Lucky Country, the United States, also champion trumpet-blowers till history began to mute their blast a couple of decades ago. What gives me hope for Australia, however, is that during recent years men have emerged who are aware of our faults and gifted enough to warn us by drawing our attention to them in highly individual and forceful ways.

Such a man is Manning Clark, the latest volume of whose *History of Australia* I've just finished reading. What both fascinates and disturbs in the picture he paints is to find that our essential characteristics are much the same as those of our mid-Nineteenth Century forbears: there are the same politicians abusing one another in larrikin style, there's the same class-consciousness in a classless society (money-consciousness might be nearer the mark), the same violence and drunkenness in the streets, at Long Bay we are building solitary confinement cells reminiscent of Port Arthur and Norfolk Island, and of course we still have that apparently insoluble problem of what to do about the Aborigines we dispossessed.

We should be deeply grateful to Manning Clark for giving us this living panorama of a developing nation, omitting none of the sweat, the wounds, the aspirations and the failures, as well as touching interludes in both high and low places. We must thank this great historian for showing us that what we were is what we are. What we may become depends on whether we are capable of waking up to ourselves.

Another man who impresses me as an exceptionally perceptive Australian — one of the most original, scintillating minds we have produced — is Barry Humphries. Ever since Sandy Stone started croaking, and Edna Everage dropped her first brick into Moonee Ponds, Barry too has been holding up a mirror for us to see ourselves. If the mirror is sometimes a distorting one, isn't distortion the prerogative of art? His film of *Bazza Mackenzie* which fell foul of the local intelligentsia — too crude — too true perhaps — went off like a cracker in darkest London where sophistication is more readily recognised. It is probably the first film conceived by an Australian and directed by another (Bruce Beresford) to show the world that we can be reckoned with as professional film-makers.

The third name I am going to invoke is that of Jack Mundey, the builder's labourer and ecologist. Mundey was the first citizen of our increasingly benighted, shark-infested city of Sydney who succeeded effectively in calling the bluff of those who had begun tearing us to bits, ostensibly in the name of progress, but in fact for their own aggrandisement, with little regard for human needs. I want to take this opportunity to salute Jack, the farm boy from Northern Queensland, who became an exceptional Australian, and incidentally that other phenomenon, a man whose sincerity has survived his rise to a position of influence.

So, with mavericks like these thrown up here and there from time to time, even a pessimist like myself ought to take heart for the future. If I have qualms in the immediate present, it is because any one of the three I have named has a right to be standing here in my place today. Perhaps when I go home I'll try sawing this impressive Object in four, and send a piece to each of them.

As THE Australian Labor Party revved itself up for its first electoral battle as a Government using the slogan *Go Ahead*, its leader Prime Minister Gough Whitlam sought endorsement from artists, writers, academics and sporting personalities in a rally on 13 May at Sydney's Opera House. Leading figures included Professor Manning Clark, poet Judith Wright, painter Lloyd Rees, playwright David Williamson, Aboriginal leader Shirley Smith, and actors John Bell and Kate Fitzpatrick. White, the main speaker, won the heart of a capacity crowd of three thousand. On the way home Judith Wright warned White, 'Once you put your foot on the flypaper you'll never shake it off'.

One year later in a letter to Prime Minister Whitlam, Patrick White said he would withdraw his support for the ALP if Whitlam went ahead with the contracts to mine sand on Fraser Island off the Queensland coast. Fraser Island had been the imaginative landscape for *A Fringe of Leaves* (1976). Whitlam was conciliatory. But it was Liberal Prime Minister Fraser who eventually revoked the export licences for the sand.

With Whitlam

1974

Prime Minister, ladies and gentlemen. It's a double privilege to be speaking here today. In the first place, I was a friend and supporter of the architect who conceived this noble building, who was driven away by Those Who Know Better before he had a chance of finishing his work. Today I am here in support of a man with similar aims whom we must not *allow* to be sacrificed as Utzon was. Both Utzon and Whitlam are men of vision who build for the future while not losing sight of the everyday details, as Utzon's domestic architecture in his native Denmark shows, and Whitlam's concern for the humbler members of society. As an artist, I am impressed by the Whitlam Government's recognition of creative endeavour and its practical encouragement of our artists to a degree no previous Australian Government has dared. This is one very substantial reason why I support the Government, and why, I believe, *most* of my fellow artists do. So today I am not talking to artists, rather to those who are not creative themselves, thousands of thoughtful people throughout Australia for whom the life of the imagination — books, painting, music, theatre — plays a very important part, and without which, existence would be drab indeed.

Some of you to whom I am speaking may be in a quandary over how to cast your vote — as I too found myself in a quandary at a certain point in the post-Menzies era. Brought up in the Liberal tradition, I realized we had reached the stage where a change had to be made — that we must cure ourselves of mentally constipated attitudes, heave ourselves out of that terrible stagnation which has driven so many creative Australians to live in other parts of the world. Whether we shall bring back these refugees is doubtful, but to offer an intellectual climate from which others won't feel the need to escape is most important and necessary, and this is what the Whitlam Government is trying to do. I support it also for its genuine efforts to alleviate poverty, and its attempts to come to grips with that most complex of all our problems, the Aborigines, both tribal and urban. I think we have come at last to understand the important part spiritual association plays in the lives of Aborigines in their original tribal surroundings. I hope we are beginning to realize the importance of these associations in the lives of white communities, particularly in the more neglected suburbs of our cities, and that the wholesale uprooting of human beings without regard for their feelings can have the most distressing psychological effects. The Whitlam Government, I believe, recognizes and respects the rights of the defenceless to a degree that the Opposition, with its subservience to monied interests, cannot pretend to emulate.

As for the world scene, it isn't possible for heads of states, or diplomats, to espouse causes as passionately as your and my individual conscience is free to embrace them, whether it be that of Israel, Greece, South Africa, Chile, or those countries of Eastern Europe where the majority is not at liberty to speak its mind, but I am confident that the Whitlam Government will lead us through the labyrinth of foreign affairs more wisely than any other political combination offering itself at this election. Certainly the Prime Minister on his visits overseas has conducted himself with more dignity and to greater purpose than his predecessors, dropping their crummy jokes in Washington and London, giving the impression they were representing some nation of rustic clowns. If I have not mentioned inflation it is because I am not competent to approach the subject. I'd only like to point out that it is something *inherited* by the Labor Government, a sickness raging in all but the most primitive countries, from which it will take years to recover; above all it is not, as the Opposition often implies, a virus capriciously injected into us by wicked Mr Whitlam and his Ministers.

These are my personal views on why we should continue to support Labor. I leave it to the Prime Minister to give you the last word on his policy.

AFTER BEING awarded the Nobel Prize and nominated Australian of the Year, White received many invitations from all parts of the world to speak. He refused all, except one to open the Henry Lawson Festival of Arts in the small New South Wales town of Grenfell — Lawson's birthplace. On that sunny Saturday morning of the Queen's birthday weekend, at the corner of Main and Forbes Streets, White climbed onto the tray of a parked lorry and addressed the crowd.

Poor Henry Lawson

1974

IN A WAY I am here today under false pretences. I'm hardly a festival addict nor can I claim to be an authority on the work of Henry Lawson *. But I felt I owed it to Grenfell, as you once honoured me with an award and besides I've had the recurring urge to take another look at a country town, in this case the birthplace of a man I feel I understand instinctively — perhaps better than some of the authorities who have written about him.

Lawson strikes me as being an extremely complex character under his deceptively simple 'Australian' surface — a tortured manic depressive soul like many other creative artists. I know this is an unfashionably romantic view of the creative artist, but I think the fashionable opinion has been developed largely by intellectuals with little of the artist in them. Believe me, the creative artist does live under enormous stress, which drives many of us to drink or drugs in order to wring out the ultimate meaning, and I cannot see that it will ever be otherwise unless the arts die an unnatural death.

One of the things which particularly distressed Henry was the grey monotony of Australian life at the period at which he lived. He made two frustrated attempts to escape, once to New Zealand and once to England. I can understand this perfectly. I too, in my youth, was driven to jump over blank walls of misunderstanding with which I was surrounded, though at that time I was certainly only a potential artist.

Henry, like many others, found he couldn't escape. He was driven back, I suspect, as I was by glimmers of remembered landscape, by scents and sounds from hot days — drawn, not necessarily 'back to the womb', to quote the frequent accusation, but to childhood, the source of creation, when perception is at its sharpest.

Again Henry found it didn't entirely work out. At least he enjoyed during his lifetime the benefit of popularity with a large reading public, even if it didn't bring him spiritual content. That is something which perhaps we manic-depressives can never enjoy.

Henry had personal friends, too — often injudiciously chosen — those phoney bohemians and bad poets of the day, chasing after Pan at Lane Cove with artificial vine leaves in their hair (they lived before the age of plastic). Sometimes Henry fell, and sometimes his friends picked him up — but not always. (Personally I divide friends into two categories: those who would pick me up when they find me lying in the gutter and those who would step over the body, pretending it wasn't there).

In spite of friends, many without a doubt sincere, there was no one in the end to close Henry's eyes. He died alone, in that seedy cottage at Abbotsford.

He was a born loser. He lived alone, and I am not ignoring his family, a long suffering wife, the mates, the *Bulletin* patrons, Angus & Robertson — the lot. At the end of his tether he once protested, 'I should have been a woman!' Surely a cry of anguish in those aggressively blokey days? Even more ironical now, when so many women are clamouring to be accepted as men.

One wonders how Henry would have reacted to life in Australia at the present time, with a Government which has set out to make the lot of the artist an easier one, and an annual festival of the arts in his name to help dispel the myth of deadly Australian country towns. Perhaps his tortured soul would have responded. Or would he have been strong enough to endure those other stresses to which we are subjected now, when an artist is expected to play, in addition to his vocational role, that of politician, diplomat, film star, academic, free psychiatrist, prophet, and what have you?

Poor Henry! He might have been worse fragmented, as, indeed, many of us are.

But if ghosts do haunt, I like to think he sometimes strolls around from those old material haunts of his, George Street and the Circular Quay, as far as that great shrine at Bennelong and down Main Street, Grenfell in festival time. I believe he might appreciate the attempts which are being made in Australia at last to celebrate the creative spirit.

I hope these few words will be considered 'opening' enough for your Festival, and that you will now feel free to enjoy yourselves. Thank you.

TO MARK the sacking of the Whitlam Labor Government by the Governor-General Sir John Kerr on 11 November the previous year, a meeting was organised at Sydney Town Hall by Citizens For Democracy — a group campaigning for a new constitution, including a Bill of Rights, which would break all ties with the British monarchy and establish Australia as a republic. White, a long-time republican and supporter of Gough Whitlam and the Australian Labor Party, delivered a speech from the balcony to those gathered below in Sydney Square.

Kerr and the Consequences

1976

 F_{ELLOW} CITIZENS ... 11 November 1975 — the day illusionists would like to persuade us to forget, and which the more realistic among us are still tormented by remembering. Whatever one's political colour, whatever one's attitude to an event many of us consider arbitrary and cynical, we are surely all agreed that we cannot run the risk of having it happen again. Whether we have a monarchy or a republic is for the moment of secondary importance — though time and the laws of history will probably give us a republic. What we must have with as little delay as possible is a trustworthy constitution. Without this, doubts will continue to breed and gnaw, encouraging cynicism and hypocrisy throughout our Australian community.

Whichever side we are on, and whatever our views on what happened just a year ago, I believe we might achieve something positive by making 11 November a day of moral stocktaking. The days of saying, 'Oh, I'm not political — I couldn't care less — I vote informal' — one would like to think that sort of thing is past. Nothing has ever been got by turning the back — except perhaps a vicious stab. The great issues concern us all — whether you are of those original components of the Australian nation, the Aborigines, or Anglo-Saxons and Celts, or you Europeans and Asians of today, who are helping us create a rich and various civilisation. We, this polyglot, but one hopes, responsible citizenry, must have our say when it comes to making the really important decisions which will confront us in the near future. If not, we must demand our say.

What I am about to suggest may not at first appear to the

point. But everything interlocks. So give it your deepest thought. Australia holds the key to immense power — the power for good or the power for evil — in its mineral wealth. The choice which has to be made cannot be made by those who are self-seeking, or a people politically distraught and insecure. Money made us as Donald Horne has pointed out with such relevance; it could *un*-make us far more quickly if we let ourselves be rushed like greedy, thoughtless antipodean innocents towards the great uranium bonanza.

This is where we the citizenry must have our say. Perhaps we can play a more positive part than those with heady visions of power and material enrichment. You who have most to lose, you on whom the nation depends for its continuance, may possibly think more objectively and soberly. *But first we must feel secure in our constitution.* This must be a priority. Otherwise, it seems to me this democracy of ours will remain an illusion floating on rhetoric, and the future could well have to offer, not the Good Life to which we aspire, but a devastated waste, for the whole world as well as for ourselves — the responsible ones. I present to you the following resolution: We Australian citizens meeting together for the first anniversary of the dismissal of an elected Australian government express our continuing concern and outrage at the event of 11 November 1975 and our firm determination to help ensure that such events will never occur again.

To COINCIDE with the Queen's visit, Citizens For Democracy organised protest rallies around Australia. White spoke at the Brisbane rally, University of Queensland on 7 March. At the Sydney Town Hall rally the following evening speakers included writers Faith Bandler, Frank Hardy, Donald Horne and poet Les Murray. White delivered a slightly amended version of his Brisbane speech to wild applause from a crowd that overflowed the main hall.

Later in the year White's play *Big Toys* was performed. His novel *A Fringe of Leaves* had been published a year earlier.

Citizens for Democracy

1977

IT GIVES ME great pleasure to be here in a city I know not so much in this century as the last. I have felt very close to its beginnings, just as I have lived intimately, painfully — in a creative sense — with the Queensland landscape. I believe that geography as well as money — with due respect to my friend Donald Horne — is what makes us, so, for that reason, through personal experiences in your landscape, I can say I feel close to you.

That does not prevent me feeling rather unhappy at having to expose my personal opinions on public occasions, a function which does not come naturally to me. If I have done so occasionally in recent years, it is because I have felt it my duty.

A conservative friend said to me the other day: 'You've changed. Have you lost your basic integrity?' I would like to quote from the poet William Blake in answering this: 'Is he honest who resists his conscience only for the sake of present ease or gratification?' Present ease and gratification — these seem the extent of our aims and ambitions in Australia today — or at least Australia as it has been run since the ubiquitous event of 11 November 1975, when an elected Government with democratic ideals and achievements — which still had the confidence of the House of Representatives — was dismissed through a sly collusion between the Monarch's representative and an ambitious caretaker. Care for what? Privilege and the established order. That this must never happen again is why we are gathered here tonight.

In the past I was innocent enough to believe that our constitution along with the Monarch's representative were trustworthy. Of course many of those representatives showed themselves to be most honourable, concerned men. But when maggots begin to appear on the meat, you have got to look at the fly-proof safe. That we should revise the constitution seems obvious. How we should change it I leave to experts like Bill Hayden, Donald Horne and others to tell you.

But I am fitted to speak, I like to think, on how our hearts, minds, our way of life should change before we can have the Australia we want. I am an artist. I think I can safely say that the majority of my fellow artists in Australia feel as I do — that the creative arts can only survive if we are politically creative as well. The Whitlam era, particularly the inspiring figure of Gough Whitlam himself, gave us this hope — which was so abjectly destroyed on November 11, 1975.

To bring it all back to a personal level, I am also a man of divided loyalties. Brought up partly in Australia after the First World War, partly in England (school and university) in the Twenties and Thirties, I can see both points of view. I have been torn apart many times over, tossed on waves of sentimentality, almost seduced by tempting offers. Above all we must not allow ourselves to be seduced, particularly in the next few days in Brisbane and elsewhere.

Let me give you a picture of myself, an adolescent schoolboy taken to a performance of an Agatha Christie play at the Haymarket Theatre, London, in, I think, 1927. It was a memorable occasion with Charles Laughton on stage. What we did not know was that the King and Queen would be present in a box — George V, a withdrawn, sober figure, and the more overtly theatrical Queen Mary in full panoply of tiara, pearl dog-collar, stomacher of diamonds. The Royal box became the play for this adolescent as well as many adolescent adults in the audience. But we grow up, don't we? Sometimes I wonder — but continue hoping.

What I am trying to say is that we must not be blinded by the theatre of pomp and circumstance on which our social structure in Australia continues to depend — on an outmoded constitution, outmoded Governor-General and cohorts of supporting knights, some of them on the distinctly murky side. What can it mean today to Australians of European origin (excepting those who have been enlisted into those same cohorts of knights), what can it mean to younger generations of British descent? I would venture to say very little. Just as it meant nothing to me after I had thrown off adolescence and started to develop a character of my own.

I have supported the Labor Party for some years now, and I shall continue to do so because as far as I can see, it has more to offer to the most Australians. There are probably those here tonight who are not of the same political persuasion, but if we are here at all I think it is because we are in search of truth and honesty. Well, we shall need every bit of honesty and moral strength we can muster if we are to face the future honourably — not only our pressing constitutional question, but the greatest issue of any time, that of uranium and atomic power.

Some of us say: 'Ah, but we shall sell it only to those who are safe'. But can we tell, since human beings are what they are, who is safe? Did not we think Kerr was safe? The Macbeth* of Yarralumla* and his lady (I think we can include her in the same package) on both of whom honours are being heaped — together with the incredible Companion of Honour to the one time caretaker*. Surely honours to the dishonourable — to the betrayers of our would-be democracy.

We are assured the Monarch has no power to regulate these embarrassments. Then would not it be better to have our own powerless figurehead rather than one in another hemisphere — a Head of State elected by the Australian people? If in some unforeseeable way our chosen man or woman should not live up to expectations, we shall have only ourselves to blame.

I ask you to consider this at a historic moment for which the media have been preparing us, not to the advantage of those who hope for progress, but to that of a reactionary Establishment. I am not afraid to confess that I am sentimental to some extent, that I value my British ties, especially to London, the great cultural centre of the world, an immense stimulus to creative art, as most Australian artists who have lived there will tell you. It would be damaging, both practically and psychologically to sever the ties with Britain completely. We need them and they need us. But we must be ourselves. We must stand on our own feet, and to do so we must have a constitution which will protect the Australian people from political conjuring tricks.

So we must resist the tentacles which have been reaching out at us through the conservative media over the last few weeks, to grapple us to the past through a variety of concepts and images — that imposing figure the Archbishop of Canterbury passing through, on another level the Queen's pathetically trivial biographer ('their domesticity is just like ours'), more sinister, in fact almost bleeped out, the announcement that Lord De L'Isle's* right-wing pressure-group is planning to open an Australian branch. Then there was the Liberal party politician urging our youth to become storm-troopers and herd us back into the dear old days of not so long ago. Astounding when the families of many Australians were herded by storm-troopers into cattle trucks, gas-chambers, ending up in the lime-pits of the Nazi campaign to extirpate European Jewry. Storm troopers! All these are forces arrayed against what I see as progress.

The Monarchy may only be symbolic, but it is a very potent symbol — by turns simple and insidious. Let us not be too easily charmed by the snapshots of domesticity — seduced by Prince Philip's fried sausage. Let us receive the Monarch with the dignity she deserves, but let us keep our heads as she walks amongst us, the myth made flesh, wearing a democratic smile.

We have grown up. You, citizens of Brisbane, have covered a great distance since those bitter beginnings at Moreton Bay emerging from the shadow of the treadmill to form the community you are in 1977. We must not turn back.

My hope is that we shall continue to evolve, all of us,

whatever our origins, colour, faith, and that we shall not be frustrated in achieving — peacefully and by the majority of consent — the goal which I see to be the only logical one — a democratic Australian republic.

A FTER HIS second electoral defeat as leader of the Australian Labor Party, Gough Whitlam resigned. Those close to him organized a thank-you farewell party for him and Margaret in Canberra on 29 January attended by two thousand people. A smattering of 'crude language' in Patrick White's eulogy, broadcast by ABC radio the following morning, provoked letters to the newspapers for and against his choice of words.

A Noble Pair

1978

I'D FIRMLY decided not to speak in public again, but when I was asked to come here tonight, I realised I must accept for what is an exceptional occasion.

I should begin by explaining why I have a fellow feeling for Gough Whitlam. Artists of any kind, if they are to amount to anything, must be prepared to take risks, to jump over the precipice every day of their lives, in their attempt to illuminate and perhaps alleviate the human dilemma. Alternately, you settle for security and the congealing comforts of tradition. No doubt this is why the creative artist in Australia has always been somewhat suspect. He troubles the spirit, the conscience, the dormant imagination of the average man. How much more deplorable, a creative politician whom the competent one sees as threatening perhaps his prosperity by offering a liberating, forward-looking way of life. This is what happened when Gough Whitlam began to dominate the scene.

A pretty dun-coloured scene it was when I returned to live in my native Australia after the Second World War, before Whitlam had emerged. Swallowing the mistake I felt I had made, I settled down to exploring in my own work Australia as I saw and sensed it. I was inclined to ignore politics, until as time went on, I realised that here was a man who might help Australia develop a civilisation of its own. I believe this is why Gough Whitlam has had such an immense appeal for so many of my fellow artists. Not only because he understands and patronises the arts, but because he is a man of creative vision. That Australia was either not worthy of, or not ready for him is by now history. They set out to destroy him, not only his enemies, but well-meaning, middle-of-the-way individuals and alas, also friends.

After I returned to this country, while I was still a detached observer-listener, one of the most familiar sounds was the heavy plop-plop of Australian bullshit. Then, this last December, I began to detect a different note — the pattering of desperate little sheep pellets, as the ever-watchful media shepherded the electoral flock to the booths and safety from one whom both the powerful and the fearful saw as the arch-dingo. Well, they had their way, but what has happened? To quote the poet Milton, 'the hungry sheep look up, but are not fed'. I'd be inclined to say bad cess* to 'em, let them enjoy the Grazier's* tender care. But, and it is a big 'but', the whole tragic situation involved the political slaughter of a great Australian.

Gough's worst flaw as a politician was that he had in him nothing of the hypocrite. He fell foul of the powerful few by trying to serve the cause of the many. He is an idealist in a world dicing with destruction for the sake of material returns. He is a great man and that is reason enough in this country for sticking him with niggling pins, slashing him with knives, cutting him down. But Gough will not lie down and die, either as a man, or as an influence.

For many of us it has been an inspiration to have lived through the Whitlam era. We shall continue to revere this concerned, this humane man and his wife Margaret. Margaret, who must have suffered more painful wounds than any other Australian politician's wife. Let us honour — I shan't say Gough's better half — not only because it is a coy and out-dated expression, but because I feel that seldom have two people been better matched.

As for the future, there has been talk that Gough may represent us at the United Nations. Whether there is any truth in that I don't know. Whether this is what he would want I wouldn't know. But to me Whitlam, more than anyone, has the stature, the intellect, the drive, the knowledge of world affairs to make himself heard at the United Nations as Australia has not been heard since the days of H.V. Evatt*.

More than anything, however, I hope for the happiness and fulfillment of two who are in the true sense a noble pair.

TWO HUNDRED librarians gathered in the Mitchell wing of the State Library of New South Wales on 19 September to open Australian Library Week. They listened to their guest of honour recall one of his childhood memories.

The Reading Sickness

1980

Mrs Wran* — Librarians — and anyone else concerned
about the future of books in a debased world...

Everybody must know by now that I can't *make* a speech,
I can only read one — which isn't inappropriate when speaking to librarians. I must say I was pretty horrified when I was
asked to do this today, but I felt I had to for several reasons.
In the first place, you librarians, as guardians of the printed
word, are such important members of society. Then I owed
it to Neville Wran for his interest in the arts. We might have
had some arch-Philistine, like others I shan't name. There are
also sentimental reasons for my being here. The first day I
made, or *read* a speech from my trembling paper, protesting
against a project which could have destroyed Centennial and
Moore Parks, the man who is now our Premier was on the
same platform. Again we were together at the Opera House
on an occasion when it seemed to many Australian artists and
intellectuals that we were really getting somewhere at last.
But we were slapped down. I like to think that before I die
we shall achieve the state I still envisage and that Nev Wran
may play an important part in accomplishing it. I know this
is supposed to be an a-political occasion, but to be realistic,
no occasion is a-political today.

Back to the Libr'y, however! I first came, or was brought
to the Mitchell when I can't have been more than three or
four years old. I had come with my parents to look at a collection of early New South Wales stamps given by my uncle
H. L. White, a philatelist, ornithologist, and bibliophile of

73

earlier this century. The collection was arranged in cabinets standing at the end of what is still the reading room of the Mitchell, before the sanctuary, as I see it. I got out of hand, as I usually did, and ran clattering over the polished floor, till the Librarian — her name was Miss Flower, I seem to remember — came up and said, 'SSShh! All the poor people are reading.' She seemed to imply they were in some way sick. I looked round and couldn't see any signs of sickness in the readers. It rather puzzled me, but she didn't give me time to work it out or ask questions. She led me up to an enormous, yellow-brown globe, and set it spinning to attract my attention. I found it momentarily of far more interest than any sheets of black old stamps or sick readers.

However, in a couple of years I too, caught the reading sickness. It was my nurse Lizzie Clark from Carnoustie, Scotland, who infected me about the age of five: *The fat cat sat on the mat* — and all that. I never looked back. I was soon in a fever — while not understanding half of what I read — but reading and reading.

It was not till much later that libraries began playing a major part in my life. I have to confess I've always been intimidated by them. The Mitchell to this day frightens me stiff. So I think you should take pains to make yourselves less frightening to those likely to be frightened. In my teens I had a great affection for the City Library because you could take the books home — those old, linted, often rather smelly volumes. In the State Library and the hallowed Mitchell, the frivolous side of my nature finds itself at variance. I can never concentrate. I am really more interested in people than ideas, so my attention continually strays from my book to the faces around me. Perhaps it's all to the good in a novelist, but it sometimes makes me feel an impostor sitting amongst so many serious people — even though we are united in our devotion to books — however different our approach and the results.

I've led a peculiar kind of life — in two hemispheres and a variety of spiritual worlds. I was sent to several schools and one university. I've had every opportunity for education, but I don't see myself as educated in the accepted sense — the

sense respected by my colonial parents, and as discussed endlessly today in the press, on the radio, and the telly. To me,
having gone through it all, real education is self-education,
though of course you've got to get the nudge from somebody.
I got very few nudges at the schools I went to, except from
a man I thought mad at the time, and realised later that his
clown's performance was that of a genius. At Cambridge the
lecturers were deadly, with the exception of one visiting
Frenchman. I more or less gave up lectures and dropped out
into the library. To give them their due, my tutors gave me
the nudge, and how grateful I am for the worlds of French
and German literature they opened up.

And this is what my perhaps boring preamble is leading
up to. I can't see that the debate by educational experts is
getting us very far. Wide and independent reading — self-
education — is what matters. And you, the librarians, are in
the best position to give a lead to confused youth. I am not
condemning our teachers, many of them genuinely dedicated
but finding it difficult to cope with over-populated classes,
in what are often antiquated schools. And when I say 'librarians', I don't mean those in a great institution like this where
you don't have the same opportunities for contact with the
ordinary or shy reader. I mean those of you in charge of sub-
urban and country libraries. You hold the balance between
hope and despair for starving intellectuals and embryo artists.
You can feed the hungry and perhaps fire imaginations by
gently suggesting.

And don't be too strait-laced. The puritan strain is one of
the great flaws in the Australian character. Some of us are
unable to distinguish between porn and bawdy — the sludge
of today and the lusty tradition of world literature, as found
in Chaucer, Shakespeare, Rabelais, to name a few exponents.
I like to remind myself of the Dorset proverb, 'God gave us
meat, we have to go to the Devil for sauce'. Good God, yes!
A spoonful of gamey sauce never harmed anybody. And how
fashions change. It's incredible to think that Flaubert's great
masterpiece *Madame Bovary* should have caused such a panic
and a court case when it appeared last century, or that *Lolita*

should have been banned only recently. I remember hearing Sydney ladies who had gone to ingenious trouble and considerable expense to smuggle Nabokov's classic satire into Australia — to enjoy a perv — afterwards protesting with disgust, 'It's so boring you can't read it!' So, let the bourgeoisie, the Festival of Light, or whomsoever, take heart. What they want to root out is in the Bible and the dictionary, anyway. The dictionary was one of my great reads as a child. Spending much of my time in the country, I might not have understood what country people were exploding about if I hadn't consulted the dictionary. My own explosive vocabulary was born in my early childhood — by life out of the dictionary.

Those early days when it is always morning! Time was endless. Even as a young man who had written a couple of insignificant novels, I felt I had endless time before me in which to write masterpieces. Now, perhaps because I am an old man, I am obsessed by the limitations of time — not only that it is running out for me personally, but for Western civilisation as a whole, and this retarded colony in particular. Whether I am deluded or not, it can only pay to pull ourselves together. Everything is happening too quickly. The pressure of circumstances and certain specific aspects of our plastic culture don't give us time to develop the art of thinking. Catchwords are popped into flabby minds by the media. The telly seduces us with hair-dos, the commentator's tie, a politician's dimple. Why, recently, our little terrier bitch got so excited, she darted forward and began smelling an alderman's dimple as he flashed it at us from the screen. Let me give you another instance of the dangers lurking in the box. I was discussing one of our politicians with a neighbour who shares my beliefs more or less. I ventured to suggest, 'He's an honest man'. My neighbour agreed, but at the same time he shook his head, 'Arr, but his image — his image won't get him *anywhere*!' In other words, it is not principles, sincerity, but the superficialities which count — the avalanche of sentimentality and technicoloured dishonesty. Unless we cultivate the habit of consulting the books in our libraries — unless we search and sift — *toughen our minds* — I feel we are lost — we cannot hope to decide for ourselves whether we really believe what the Americans, the British, the Soviet or even some of our more abysmal politicians, and of course our newspaper proprietors, tell us we should.

The blight from the box is one of the most pernicious Twentieth Century diseases. If ever I appear on television, not from choice, but during some crisis when I feel I have to, immediately people I pass in the street start turning on sentimental smiles, even though I know the majority do not really approve of what I tell them. They probably wouldn't have understood the language I speak, anyway. Quite often when I talk to children, even adults, they look at me in blank surprise because I don't trot out the half-a-dozen telly cliches — for the most part gifts from our American overlords — with which so many Australians communicate today — when the minerals of language and thought are here in the libraries, waiting to be mined, as potentially as important for our future as uranium.

The wisdom which surpasses money, cars, swimming pools, and sport...It seems to me when I look around and see children toiling on the playing fields almost any day of the week that sport plays the major part in Australian education. A mother tells me, 'Oh well, if my children don't play sport they won't get good passes'. I like to think — I do believe that librarians can combat to a great extent this pathetic attitude. You're in a better position than the teacher, because we're all of us a bit averse to teacher and school, and we're not inclined to think of you as crypto-teachers because your approach makes us feel more adult. I'm convinced it will be sharp wits — moral strength — not muscle — perhaps not even armaments — that will save us in a grim future. You librarians can offer us an antidote to mindlessness — and to worse, the dishonesties undermining society in every walk of life, every class of a supposedly classless democracy — together with the childish, false optimism of jingle-land.

Time is running out! Even if the fat cat is still sitting on the mat, he won't be there much longer. It may appear a hopeless mission trying to stave off the collapse of a great civilisation — particularly to shore up one like our own, still struggling to emerge from the colonial mists. But who knows, we may succeed in building something better through our collaboration — you the guardians of the printed word — we, the writers — all those who read and think for themselves — and any politician in whom we can still have faith.

AUSTRALIAN BOOK WEEK was opened with a Literary Awards Dinner on 10 October. Patrick White was invited to present the winning writers with their awards and speak about his own writing, in particular the autobiography he was working on.

His novel *The Twyborn Affair* had been published the previous year.

Truth and Fiction

1980

WHAT I'M going to try to talk about is how the pursuit of truth differs in factual writing and fiction, according to my own experience. As a writer of fiction it's a difference I've only recently had to face up to. I've never wanted to write an autobiography, trundling over a long life introducing the celebrities one meets for five minutes and most of whom aren't all that interesting anyway.

Instead I decided to do a self-portrait to try to show what I *think* I am and how it came about. It's the kind of writing which survives only if it is the quintessence of truthfulness. I should say the most difficult kind of factual writing. As one goes along one wonders: is the novelist in me taking over? Shall I perhaps overdo the flaws in my anxiety to portray the real person? At the period when I was growing up we tended to regard reality as predominantly sordid. Certainly it is easier and more drastic to record, say — the cry of horror as a cockroach flies into the open mouth than to convey the strength of spirit in Ayia Sophia, Constantinople, after centuries of humiliation under Islam.

A couple of years ago I had a conversation with the English painter Bridget Reilly, who confirmed some of my doubts. 'You run the risk of painting White blacker than he is.' I remember another of her remarks during that same conversation. 'I started a house and studio in the South of France thinking I could paint there in detachment and ideal surroundings. But you can't. Even abstract painters can't afford to sever their roots.' This is what I think I sensed before returning to live in Australia after Hitler's War. Australian expatriate writers and artists in general, eventually starve in the absence of their natural sustenance.

Journalists are a different breed. Their roots are air roots. I often envy them their freedom as I sit endlessly at my desk, my bronchial tubes filling up as I work. Anyway, I came back, and wrote novel after novel. Whether it's been a waste of time, or whether they convey the truth I was searching for, only time, not Professor Kramer*, will show.

And now towards the end of my life I am doing this dangerous thing, the self-portrait. Recently I read a potted, one volume version of George Sand's *Ma Vie*. As a fundamentally sincere woman she couldn't help telling the truth. But a lot is left out — anyway in the abridgement — perhaps the rest is scattered through the 20 vols I haven't read. The impression one gets is of a watercolour of the kind of woman Courbet might have painted in oils — one of those *demoiselles* stretched dreaming on a river bank her necklaces of Venus fully exposed. In his biography of George Sand, drawing on the opinions and experiences of those who knew her, André Maurois probably gives us the actual woman — a great force and sounding board at the time when she lived — like most of us full of obsessions and delusions. A lot of her strength came from devotion to her native province of Berry. She was the greatest advocate for roots. This is not intended as a vulgar joke at George's expense, but as a plea to artists to cling to the soil from which they grew — even if it is the grit of Melbourne's pavements — or the garbage of Sydney's gutters.

Actually George, in spite of her reputation as a female Don Juan, was not so hot where sexuality entered in. She was less the passionate lover than an earth mother in search of the Absolute in love and faith — which she never found. But in the course of her turbulent life, as woman, man, lover, novelist and pamphleteer, political and social revolutionary, descended from royal bastards and plebeian birdsellers, she attracted many dedicated friends and equally dedicated enemies who all contribute to her portrait.

Another emancipated woman of the day, Marie d'Agoult,

Liszt's aristocratic mistress, said of George, 'She used her lovers like the chalk you write with on the blackboard, and then ground them to dust under foot'. George, though a noble soul, realised that friendship is in many ways a game of hurt for hurt. She said of Marie, 'Everything about her is artificial — teeth, breasts, aristocracy. Her financier family bought the title under the Regency.' Sounds a bit like the Colonies.

Which brings me back to what I should be talking about: fact and fiction in Australia. It has always troubled me that so many Australian novelists are content to explore an auto-biographical vein instead of launching into that admittedly disturbing marriage between life and imagination — like many actual marriages in fact — all the risks, the recurring despair, and rewards if you are lucky. Certainly most of the novels George wrote are autobiographical. But this is not what I want of our Australian novelists — writing so diligently about their Catholic youth, their Catholic lapse.

Why it recurs, I suppose, is because Australians are taught to revere the pragmatic, the documentary approach. I have a ninety-four year old aunt who used to tell her aspiring novelist nephew, 'I always feel guilty if I read a novel — because it isn't true'. (Actually what she read was mainly Ruby M. Ayres, self-confessed Queen of the Tripe-writers.) But I do think my aunt's was one of the prevailing attitudes in the past — which didn't depress or influence me because I had the good fortune to escape and spend several years of my earlier life in other parts of the world.

If George Sand has helped me out in this talk tonight, there is a book by another writer which will carry me farther into what I want to say about the difference between truth in factual writing and fiction. It is Axel Clark's biography of the poet Christopher Brennan. To me Brennan is a painfully medi-ocre poet who lived at a time when Australia was desperately in need of poetry, and culture generally. He was probably a considerable scholar — I'm not in a position to judge. As I see him his importance lay in his nonconformity, in a surreal element he added to a smug colonial society badly in need of a purge. Clark makes this clear after shovelling his way through mountains of turgid poetry. His books seem to one who is in no way a scholar a model of dogged scholarship.

But what I find most exciting about this biography is that it lights the way to fiction. It astonishes me that some novelist of Roman Catholic background, instead of writing up his own Catholic boyhood and lapse, did not seize on Brennan, a figure of doom and high tragedy — such a grand lapse from the Austral-Irish-puritan faith, into the depths of physical and spiritual squalor, and finally the almost operatic return into the bosom of his Church. Well, there it all is — still waiting for somebody.

In suggesting this I don't advocate a documentary or historical novel. Axel Clark could not have done the factual version better. Personally I tend to dislike historical novels, and have avoided writing them because of the strictures they impose on the imagination. Instead, on a couple of occasions, I have taken a historical character or moment, as starting point. I feel this is permissable if you preserve psychological credibility and respect your aesthetic principles — the fiction need not decline into romance. If, instead of writing *Voss*, I had written a novel about Leichhardt, in whose life there was no woman his obsessive equal, or if in *A Fringe of Leaves* I hadn't substituted Ellen Roxburgh for Eliza Fraser, little more than a hard-bitten shrew from the Orkneys, neither novel would have had the psychological complexities, the sensibility, and the passion I was able to explore.

But I've gone on long enough about myself. The night belongs to the prize-winners, each of whom has pursued truth and shone a light on what till now we have accepted as the forms of reality and the motives for human behaviour. If I ask you to put up with me just a moment longer, it's because I'm tempted to end on a slightly political note, though some of my friends may again accuse me of humourlessness. So many Australians are made uneasy if one feels intensely — whether in writing, life, politics. And when it comes to politics, I can't help being intensely aware of the hypocrisy, side-stepping, and arrogant disregard for truth in recent years. The voice of the Führer can be heard in the land, and unless we have in us enough passionate concern to alter course radically from the one we have been pursuing — I feel Australia could be lost.

A RARE INTERVIEW which Patrick White gave to Paul Murphy. It was filmed in Centennial Park, and broadcast by ABC-TV's *Nationwide* programme on 7 March. As so often with his public statements, it sparked a flurry of annoyance and admiration in the letters pages and columns of the newspapers.

State of the Colony

1981

Why have you chosen now to speak out against foreign interests subverting Australian independence?

Because there's evidence of it every day. And I think the newspapers tend to show us things as they want us to see them. I don't trust those who control the press. Recently a newspaper editor told me I was trying to rubbish Australia, when my aim is to help clean up some of the rubbish which prevents many Australians taking a pride in their country. It was ironic to read in an article by Guy Harriot of the *Sydney Morning Herald* that Israel must realise it is time she stood on her own feet while we are encouraged daily to snuggle closer to the Americans and the British, to accept Prince Charles as possible Governor-General, to welcome the presence of the Americans at Pine Gap, Darwin, and other points — *and* the coming of a bosom friend of Richard Nixon's to the American Embassy Canberra. I find it hard to contain my cynicism, not to say despair, at such a prospect. No wonder many of my friends say, we don't read the papers, we don't know what's going on. In some cases I feel this is because they're going along cynically with what's happening, in others they simply don't know what to believe, and are waiting for somebody to speak up for *us* — somebody not a politician.

Why are you upset by the Prince Charles for Governor-General episode? Hasn't every era enjoyed royal romance? Or do you see something sinister in it — a conspiracy to distract us from reality?

Of course it'll be used for all it's worth to distract the unfortunate British from a grim situation — unemployment and Thatcher's economic mess. Here we have it presented as a rosy *Women's Weekly* romance to lull the more soft-centred among us and again to distract attention from reality. We are encouraged to accept those tireless commuters the Royal Family — hardly a month when we're without one or other of them. At the same time a troop of noble and not so noble, but wealthy English families are buying into Australia by the hectare as though they see this reactionary colony as a convenient bolthole for them and the Monarchy should the worst happen in Britain. I don't see the Monarchy as relevant to most Australians of today. Something for those of an older generation of Anglo-Saxon origins, and sentimental nostalgia for more recent migrants. Some of the Aboriginal leaders have accepted honours doled out to them ostensibly by the Monarch, but I expect even they see the Crown as a super symbol of those who seized their tribal lands and to this day deny them equal rights with the white usurpers. The British Monarchy means little to Australians from Southern Europe. Italians and Greeks, the so-called ethnics I know best, have memories of crowned heads they're glad to be rid of. I'd say almost all Austral Greeks would welcome an Australian Republic, the exceptions being some of the monied ones at the top who were on with the Greek Junta when the Colonels were in power and see a British Monarchy as protecting their interests. Asians, I'd say, couldn't care less about the Queen of England and her heir. And yet we are having this Monarchy foisted on us by a wealthy Establishment who got control through the Kerr Coup.

You seem to be saying that all Australian artists and intellectuals have been neutered by five years of Fraserism. Has Fraser lulled the Australian intelligentsia?

Not so much Fraser, though he *is* the archphilistine who neither understands nor sees much need for the arts. We have been lulled by Kerr's successor, the present Governor-General*, a model servant of the Crown who has done more than any body to undermine the Republican Movement by distributing orders and titles to artists and intellectuals whose vanity does not allow them to refuse. One very cunning ploy is the honorary degree to be conferred on Prince Charles by Monash, our most progressive university. It's part of a 'battle operation' — Prince Charles's own words in describing his engagement to Lady Di. In Australia too there is a military precision about the course of events — the succession of royal visits, and that high-ranking officer Lord Carrington, an expert meddler in colonial affairs, supervising operations, just as Lord De L'Isle hovered at the time of the Kerr Coup.

You sound romantically tied to the Whitlam days. But weren't there good reasons why the Australian people rejected Whitlam in 1975 (inflation, unemployment etc.) which override Whitlam's concern for the arts. Could you be accused of elitism in your approach?

Admittedly there was inflation and unemployment in the Whitlam era, but inflation and unemployment were a worldwide sickness, and are worse in Australia today. Of course Whitlam tried to introduce too many reforms too soon, which alarmed conservative Australians and made them fear for their money. They were not so concerned for the welfare of the less well-off, as they aren't today, when increasing numbers of people have a heartrending struggle to make ends meet. I can see this while doing my shopping in an unfashionable part of Sydney, from talking to people, and from an association of many years with the Smith Family*. I do know something about the needy in my own city, where at the other end of the scale the affluent are bloating themselves by overeating. I am not a writer with purely intellectual and aesthetic concerns, a romantic elitist yearning for the Whitlam days. History has flowed on. I get many a slap in the face from the backwash.

You sound full of despair. In the 1950s, when artists like you felt the inexorable onset of philistinism, many left the country. Is that an option you'd consider?

In my youth I stayed away, having experienced Australian philistinism. I returned after World War II for various reasons, some of them ignoble, such as the desire to fill my belly. I have known what it is to go hungry. Often in those years after my return I felt I'd taken the wrong step — there were many humiliations — but you can't keep running away for ever. Also, the number of people who share my interests was increasing, and this, after all, is my country. I intend to see things out, doing what I can when I see my way. But I can't deny I'm full of the despair you detect.

Has this despair reflected itself in your recent writing? Have you considered writing more journalistic/political/satirical works?

Yes, it *has* been reflected in my writing, because as I grow older I am more acutely conscious of the tragi-comic farce in which we are playing parts. I expect I shall continue to write satirical works. I shall not become a journalist because you have to train for that from the beginning. And I don't want to become a politician. I'm an artist. I haven't enough vanity in me to become a politician or any kind of public figure. (As an artist of course I'm to some degree vain, or I shouldn't be one.) But public figures must be unquenchably vain. They must also be able to disguise disgust and suppress laughter.

You seem to have been very politicised over the last ten years, first with the Whitlam ascendancy, then with the return of conservative rule. Is it a good thing for artists to become so political?

In one way it's bad for artists to become political, but it's also unavoidable if they don't want to become museum pieces, stuffed emblems which are convenient for the Establishment to use. But today there's a political reason underlying everything that is done. So how can you ignore this. Music is supposed to be apolitical. Recently I was asked to become patron of a music organisation formed in London to help young Australian musicians living in England. I was told it would strengthen the ties between our countries. I had to point out that their aim was political and that as an Australian Republican I thought these ties should be cut. Yes, it was during the Whitlam era that I became political, first from exhilaration, then through a sense of outrage. People began to accuse me of being a traitor to my class, when I like to see any artist as classless — a seeing eye or recording angel. The other day I came across vague reference to my resignation from the Order of Australia in an article promoting the new 'patriotism'. Without explanation of why I did so, it made me look capricious, unreasonable — rubbishing Australia again. Well, this is how it happened. When the Order was inaugurated under Whitlam, I was offered the AC (Companion of the Order of Australia), but hesitated to accept because I felt that, as a writer, my teeth would be drawn. The Governor-General* of the day told me I would 'ruin everything' if I refused, so I agreed to take it. After Kerr himself had ruined everything in the opinion of many of us by sacking the elected Government, I returned the Order, as did Dr Coombs, an exemplary Australian (nothing two-faced about Nugget) who has worked more than anyone to see justice done by the Aborigines. In recent times the AC, our highest honour, has been awarded to a Japanese businessman, surely making a mockery of what was a noble concept?

If you had to sum up with what's wrong with the scene in Australia at the moment, what main points would you make?

I see us making a mockery of patriotism by cheap trumpet-blowing, silly jingles, and trying to snaffle Prince Charles for Governor-General. The Prince is recommended to us as a Christian gentleman, which perhaps he is, but ironic when meant to impress a country where only a token Christianity is observed, and Church leaders align themselves with some pretty dubious secular knights by accepting titles. Would Christ have approved of their worldliness or the big business their Churches have become? Would He have approved of lawyers who observe the letter of the Law while ignoring its spirit? At every level of the power structure we are missing our chances to create a great independent democracy of the South. Everything is done to distract our attention from reality — through royal weddings, titles, the advertising of unnecessary goods, expensive cars, the soporific thud of the cricket ball, gladiatorial displays by steak-fed footballers. Sport could sink us — so many Australians think of nothing else. Reality is the rape of this country for its mineral wealth regardless of the shambles we'll be left in when foreign interests are appeased and the dollars blown. Reality as it could and should be is justice both moral and material for the many — in an *independent* democracy — which has learnt to defend *itself,* by armaments and manpower only if necessary, but what is more essential, by sharpened minds.

Do you find that journalists and others wilfully misrepresent you?

Perhaps not wilfully, unless those who see me as part of the 'Communist menace'. I think they misunderstand me inevitably, as it is difficult to understand a person of any complexity without a lot of delving. Even people who've known me all my life don't really know me. I've written a book trying to show what I am. But I'm here to talk about the state of the colony, not myself.

Do you regard yourself as in step with modern times? Do you hanker after days which cannot return?

What I deplore about this country is that *those who are running it* are not in step with modern times. They would like us to remain the Grazier's reactionary colonial sheep run, they yearn to creep back inside Big Mummy's cosy womb and lie there blissfully oblivious of the demands of life, the advance of history. The flow of history is what we have to face and adapt ourselves to. The adjustments we shall have to make may be pretty agonising. But they will have to be made. Otherwise, when our British and American overlords have faded away, and the bull-dust has cleared, Australia may be remembered by relics of a quaint, abortive culture in the museums of *Japan's* colonial empire — a fate to which our politicians are condemning us by considering their own immediate interests instead of the future of an entire nation.

JACK MUNDEY, together with his colleagues Owens and Pringle, had led the Builders Labourers' Federation during the early 1970s in actions sympathetic to urban environmental issues. But they were ousted by a tougher leader, Norm Gallagher, who foresaw a greater future for the BLF in co-operation with developers. White, an admirer of Mundey, wrote this Open Letter to the Australian Congress of Trade Unions which was meeting in Sydney in September.

A few years later White commented to a journalist, 'I think any story written about Jack Mundey should be entitled *The Wasted Australian*. I consider him to be a great man whose talents have been wasted.'

Jack Mundey and the BLF

1981

SEVEN YEARS ago Mundey, Pringle, Owens and their supporters in the BLF were expelled from the union on the grounds that they had maladministered and misappropriated union funds and property. It was in the days of the Askin government. Premier Askin was bitterly opposed to the Green Bans and had come to an agreement with his cronies the developers. His Minister for Planning and Development Sir John Fuller admitted when the Green Bans were lifted from Victoria Street in 1975 that there had been collusion between himself, Norm Gallagher, Federal Secretary of the BLF, and Theeman, one of the leading developers. Amongst other things, the NSW BLF under Mundey had been opposed to the development of high rise in Woolloomooloo, an area which they felt should be developed in more down to earth style for lower income citizens. The Federal BLF began moving in. Gallagher never properly understood, or did not want to understand, that Green Bans were never imposed unless a request had been made by a delegation of local residents. But the NSW branch was duly throttled by a concerted opposition. As for the charges of dishonesty these were twice dismissed, in 1974 by Judge Holland of the Equity Division of the Supreme Court, who recommended that a new union ticket should not be issued in NSW, and again in 1978 when the full bench of the Federal Court (Judges Sweeney, Evatt, and Keeley) unanimously cleared Mundey, Pringle, and Owens. Gallagher announced he would ignore the Federal Court's decision. Meanwhile Mundey, Pringle and Co are still denied the right to work in the industry that concerns them.

I first met Mundey when the middle-class neighbourhood in which I live was threatened by Lewis and Shehadie's proposal to turn the area into a venue for the Olympic Games. This would have involved Moore Park as part of the plan, the working class suburbs on the other side, as well as our unique Centennial Park, which would have been more or less destroyed by freeways and an Olympic pool at the southern end. I consider the parks were saved principally by the efforts of Mundey and the BLF and Professor Neil Runcie the economist of the University of NSW. Mundey struck me at once as a remarkably charismatic character when we spoke at a rally in the Town Hall. We spoke again on another occasion in the Wayside Chapel, with Theeman's thugs jeering at us from the balcony, as we took part in the battle to save Victoria Street. Through Mundey and the NSW BLF Woolloomooloo was undoubtedly saved from highrise. If things went wrong at the Rocks it was because the forces of reaction had strengthened their hand. The Rocks area today is not what the resident action group, its sympathisers, and the NSW BLF had envisaged.

Why is Mundey anathema to the establishment at either end of the political and social structure? I think it is because he is one of those Australian mavericks with true creative gifts. And real creative gifts are feared, whether by the capitalist establishment of the Fraser Government, or at the other end the cut and dried union establishment. I have been asked why I support a commo* like Mundey — or am I a commo myself? I support him because, apart from the fact that he has been cleared in two superior courts of law, he has shown me that he is an exceptional Australian, that he has so much to offer his country if only the plodding majority would see it. I am not a communist. I have never belonged to any political party. I don't belong to the Labor Party though I have supported it for some years, and shall continue to do so unless things go very wrong. I am not a politician who can lose votes by supporting Mundey. That's great. I've never belonged to a union, not even the Fellowship of Australian Writers. I've always

preferred to go it alone, do things my own way. I see Mundey
as a man of vision, as he was seen by the British economist
and international environmentalist Barbara Ward on one of
Mundey's visits overseas. This exceptional woman, who unfor-
tunately died of cancer a few months ago, saw, as Mundey
does, that unless we protect the rain forests and plant life,
which preserve the band of moisture necessary to life on this
planet, we are lost. Just as Mundey realises that if we rape
the Australian soil for the minerals in it and hand them over
to those who are greedy for them as Mistranthony advocates
— safeguards and all — we are only helping to destroy by more
violent means the planet on which we live. So I see Mundey
as a positive, not a divisive force, as he proved when he united
individuals of all classes in this divided democracy. It will
be to our shame if we don't give him another chance to prove
himself — which is why I am here today doing what doesn't
come naturally to me — above all trying to expiate my personal shame for much of what happens in Australia today.

PEOPLE For Nuclear Disarmament was founded in 1981 in Melbourne. Despite ill health, White went to the inaugural meeting on 21 October. He became a sponsor along with poet Judith Wright and others, and gave the keynote address to a gathering of more than a thousand people — the first of many impassioned pleas in public for the anti-nuclear cause. He was sixty-nine years old.

The publication a week earlier of his self-portrait *Flaws in the Glass* had drawn strong reactions and was described as 'the literary event of the year'.

And if a Button is Pressed

1981

As I'M grabbed by old age with its various geriatric ailments, it worries me that I can't get on with my work as a writer. What I see as creative writing has been my life. Political issues have entered into it only in recent years. I've always resented this while going along with it when I've seen it to be necessary. As one who isn't essentially a political animal I grew particularly resentful when the great nuclear debate started nudging my conscience.

The implications of nuclear warfare are so immense that it's tempting to turn our backs — to persuade ourselves it can't concern Australia. Until, if we're honest, we have to admit that beside this global issue *nothing else matters.* What work of fiction, written in these circumstances, can seem anything but trivial? What of the children you beget if their legacy is one of anguish and ashes? As for money — will it make life any easier for those fossicking among the ruins? Wealth *shouldn't* ease the conscience of those who supplied the destroyers with uranium.

This is what we must face in Australia and other once remote corners of the earth, as the American and Soviet leaders rush us towards what could be global extinction. It's becoming increasingly obvious that we can't depend on Heads of State. Reading about the recent CHOGM conference (Commonwealth Heads of Government Meeting) — that feast of words and catering — one was hardly aware of the nuclear threat hanging over us. There were formal discussions on help to under-developed countries — whose needs will be far greater if the nuclear war is allowed to develop. In a sense those important persons at the conference were as insouciant as the decent extrovert Australian jogging away his long weekend while the nuclear holocaust is preparing.

Fortunately the people of the world — at any rate those in Europe, the US and Britain — the ones most likely to suffer from their leaders' power games, and who can't expect the well-appointed bunkers of the wealthy and important — the *ordinary* people are banding together in increasing numbers to call for *nuclear disarmament*. In joining them, Australian men and women of good will could lift themselves out of the colonial rut. We might make a far more positive contribution than jogging along behind CHOGM with its bland plans for the betterment of man when a man-devised plan exists to destroy the greater part of human life.

There is of course the unpredictable Soviet with its military incursions. But has the capitalist West ever given the Soviet reasonable proof of its good intent? Have we ever tried to reach the conscience, not of the party leaders, but the *Russian people*? If the capitalist West, investing trillions in promoting consumer goods — appliances, cigarettes, the plastic trash we seem to think necessary to our way of life — spent a tithe of this in trying to communicate with the Russian *people,* we might break through. No doubt many will say impossible. But after all we do communicate with those behind the lines in wartime. Why not give it a go in what passes for peace? Otherwise we leave our fate in the hands of ruthless politicians and transnational business. What could be more ruthless than the minister who proposes to *fly* uranium out of Australia when its shipment has been blocked?

Cynicism abounds around the world. Here is a point to illustrate it: 30% of West Germany's uranium, together with Sweden's and Finland's, is enriched by the Soviet. With all these cosy links, and Australia's proposal to supply Finland with yellow-cake, surely our talk of safeguards has the sound of claptrap. We shall be as safe as we were in the days when Hitler struck up an alliance with Stalin.

If we can't look to our leaders, where can we put our faith? We, the people of the world, *may* hold the key to the situation if we can only unite — trade unions, families, artists and intellectuals, and most important in Australia, the Aborigines to whom many of the mining sites belong by tradition. We are in it together, all classes, all colours. We must resist the lust for undue wealth, which is what inspires our politicians, regardless of the effect this lust will have on future generations — if there *is* a future.

Often when I'm walking through my local park and listen in to the runners whose sole concern seems to be their running times, when I watch parents strolling with their children, so many of them around the ages of 2-3-4, and the trendy rich tearing towards social engagements in the latest of their exotic cars, I wonder how many of them pause to think that time may be running out. Or are they lulled by the thought that Lucky Australia is too far away — it can't happen here. When everything can and does happen where *you* are. It is demonstrated over and over — by the mounting violence in a once comparatively benign country, outbreaks of gang warfare amongst desperate adolescents, bombs, arson, practically a murder a minute, and near murder in our gladiatorial sports. It is happening. And if a button is pressed by either of the major powers in another hemisphere, inaugurating the greatest mayhem in history, destroying or maiming human beings in Europe and that other battlefield the US, you can be sure the Lucky Country will not remain untouched. Not at once perhaps will the effect be felt. It will reach us slowly and insidiously through the polluted skies and oceans of this planet. It will reach your children. Not mine. I'm childless. But as I look around me and see these unsuspecting children, I feel they are one of *my* responsibilities in this somewhat childish country of ours.

So I urge those of you who think and feel — members of the universal family of whom I am one — to unite in resisting the nuclear madness with which certain leaders are possessed, a madness of which the Trident submarine is sufficiently concrete evidence, the long-range missiles America and the Soviet are prepared to unleash, not forgetting Cowboy Reagan's unspeakable land-based weapon, and the cold, frequently brutal commitment of Führerin Thatcher.

A lot of us remember the bombs dropped on Japan at the end of World War II. It did put an end to the war, but consider the price — the moral degradation of the victors, the most horrible deaths, deformities and suffering of the victims. And those were the horse-and-buggy days of nuclear weaponry. Today when science has perfected the techniques of destruction, nuclear warfare could mean the immediate annihilation of what we know as civilisation, followed by a slow infection of those who inhabit the less directly involved surface of this globe — as it revolves in space — swathed in its contaminated shroud.

WITH BALLOONS, banners and placards 40,000 people gathered in Sydney's Hyde Park on Palm Sunday, to be with friends and confirm their devotion to peace on earth. Respectfully, the peace demonstrators listened to star speaker Patrick White read his Open Letter from the stage. White has been a leading figure in the front line of many subsequent Palm Sunday peace marches that have attracted crowds of up to 130,000.

A Letter to Humanity

1982

FELLOW HUMAN BEINGS... My addressing you in this way could sound a bit whimsical. I do so — with good reason, I think — because an outrage against humanity has brought us here today. Nuclear war is undoubtedly the most serious issue the global family has ever had to face. After Hiroshima it should appear the most hideous to any but thoughtless minds. Fortunately, increasing numbers of human beings are becoming aware of the implications of nuclear warfare. The people of the world are disturbed by the direction in which their political mentors are leading them. There is a gathering anger. Just as the earth too, is angry. For it seems to me that the earth's erupting volcanoes and repeated earthquakes are more than coincidental in these days of nuclear tests. Australians must — a lot of us do accept the fact that the nuclear situation affects us as much as those living in the northern hemisphere. We are united by the polluted skies and oceans as well as by the earth's crust. The French nuclear tests in the Pacific should bring the future very close indeed to those Australians who would like to think their island inviolable. Many of those who have been alerted and who have come here today, either in quandary or out of conviction, see the nuclear issue as transcending party politics, class, race. It involves people of whatever religious faith or philosophical persuasion. I like to think that all of us at this demonstration are people of faith — faith in humanity — and continuing life on this abused planet. In Europe, Britain and the United States intellectuals, churchmen, scientists (in particular medical authorities) are uniting

with the man in the street to question what they see as fool-
hardiness on the part of their political leaders. Draft avoidance
by millions of young Americans is one of the most striking
symptoms of unrest, the biggest act of civil disobedience since
the end of the Vietnam War, an expressive sign of the rapidly
expanding peace movement. In June, one million are expected
to demonstrate while the UN special session on disarmament
is taking place. In many cases the reaction of these draft
resisters is moral rather than political. Nuclear disarmament
is humanity's answer to the paranoiacs and megalomaniacs,
whether American or Soviet, and our own lilliputian leaders
intent on supplying the giants with the material for global
destruction.

More than half the uranium used in West European power
plants is enriched in the Soviet Union. The first Australian
uranium destined for the Soviet Union will reach the Latvian
port of Riga later this year, be taken by train to a Soviet enrichment plant, not yet identified by our officials, then leave Lenin-
grad for its final destination, a Swedish-built nuclear power
plant in Finland. Australia has signed uranium deals with four
countries which use Soviet enrichment: Finland, West Germany, Sweden, and France. All contracts written since 1977
are held by the only two companies now producing in Australia: Queensland Mines, which owns the Nabarlek Reserve,
and has signed sales with Japan, Finland, and South Korea;
and Energy Resources of Australia, operator of the Ranger
Deposit, which has contracts with Japan, West Germany,
South Korea, the US, Sweden, and Belgium. So the governments of the world are linked by the crossthreads of a monstrous web, spun from the motives of material gain, fear and
suspicion, and in the case of the two superpowers, determination to dominate the world at whatever cost.

We talk of *safeguards* — when obsolete nuclear submarines
are to be dumped in the ocean — when American Tridents
and their Soviet counterparts will be cruising through our
waters — when the South American rivals Brazil and Argen-
tina are flat out to control the nuclear cycle and build a bomb.
In the present circumstances it isn't any wonder that coun-

tries like India and Pakistan, courted by the US and the Soviet Union, indulge in political juggling, and Israel is reduced to hijacking shiploads of material to conduct its nuclear experiments. Australia's future as uranium exporter depends on two nations in particular — Japan the samurai turned merchant — and France, whose materialist techniques in economic matters, whichever the political party in power, are far more sophisticated than our own crude game of grab. France, with unabashed cynicism, continues to explode its nuclear devices not so far distant from our Pacific seaboard. At least our government, with comparable cynicism, has asked for it. The most innocent victims of the universal swindle are those to be pitied most — the Australian Aborigines who, after the original invasion of their land, are now invaded by uranium miners who drive bulldozers across their burial grounds and sacred sites and smash or steal their sacred emblems. The Ranger Agreement was signed between our former Aboriginal Affairs Minister, Mr Viner, and four of the traditional owners of the land that was to be mined. The four who signed were bullied into it by a government which told them all the aboriginal communities had been consulted — which later proved to be untrue.

Not surprisingly, when the virtues of nuclear power are outweighed by its capacity for evil, the history of the product in Australia and its diplomatic concomitants is one of lies, hypocrisy, naivety, and ignorance. Over the years, those who governed us seem to have been at their most naive in allowing the Americans to establish their bases at North-West Cape, Nurrungar, the Omega Station in Gippsland, and most important, the CIA-controlled monitoring and information complex at Pine Gap, which those who have seen the Gil Scrine film, *Home on the Range,* will realize has played a significant part in Australia's political history — not least the episode of Sir John Kerr, claimed by the CIA as one of their so-called 'assets'. Under the spell of their American ally's advances our government appeared unaware of what they might be letting us in for. Some of the negotiations were positively light-headed. Take for instance the film-clip in which Harold Holt*, in true music-hall-style goes into a little soft-shoe shuffle as he and the American ambassador quip about peppercorn rentals. And what of the agreement by which American B52s may land at Darwin without any active concern about knowing whether they are bombed up? By now Australia has become an important nuclear target, not just the American installations, but even our cities.

The Australian people, who have been kept in the dark, will bear the brunt of a nuclear attack. *They* will be the incidental target, not the politicians in their well-planned shelters. *Nowhere* have the *people* been consulted, whether in Britain, where women have been camped all through the recent severe winter round sites prepared to receive American Cruise nuclear missiles, nor in the United States, where the Frankenstein consortium of millionaires who launched their monster Reagan — a figure from one of his own B films — listened with apparent equanimity to his suggestion that the aged should be the first out to test the effects of nuclear ash. I'd have thought the creaking monster himself might have qualified to dip his toe before anybody.

But from being the suckers of the world, the people have begun to act. Individuals who are prepared to accept their fate say to me: But what can you or I do to resist the policies of governments? I reply there are millions of you and me. Small scale passive resistance can work wonders, as some of you will have found out in your domestic lives. On a larger scale it worked in India, where the great Mahatma Gandhi won independence for his country. Let me quote you some of this great human being's own words: 'I am a Christian and a Hindu and a Moslem and a Jew. The politician in me has never dominated a single decision of mine, and if I seem to take part in politics, it is only because politics encircles us today like the coil of a snake, from which one cannot get out, no matter how much one tries. I wish therefore to wrestle with the snake, as I have been doing with more or less success consciously since 1894, unconsciously, as I have now discovered, ever since reaching years of discretion. I have been experimenting with myself and my friends by introducing religion into politics. Let me explain what I mean by religion. It is not the Hindu religion, which I certainly prize above all other religions, but the religion which transcends Hinduism, which changes one's very nature, which binds one indissolubly to the truth within and which ever purifies. It is the permanent element in human nature which counts no cost too great in order to find full expression and which leaves the soul utterly restless until it has found itself, known its Maker and appreciated the true correspondence between the Maker and itself.'

Gandhi's words are pretty hard to live up to. But through his faith he achieved what he set out to do. In these days of advanced nuclear development, *we* shall have to call on all our reserves of faith. Ah yes, some of my friends say, but what about the Russians... Perhaps it isn't generally known what the Russian Orthodox Church still means to a large percentage of Soviet citizens and that they still attend its services. You may not know of the peace movement in East Germany, where a large demo was recently organized in Dresden to commemorate the 37th anniversary of that city's destruction by British and American bombers and the deaths of 35,000 people. The gathering was sponsored by the regional head of the Protestant Church, Bishop Hempel, who proposed that East Germany should unilaterally renounce the stationing of Soviet-built nuclear missiles in its territory, and called for compulsory 'peace education' in East German schools. As the protest had an anti-Western undertone, the party has been in two minds how to proceed. At least man's conscience is still alive — men of faith — whether Russian Orthodox — East German Protestant — the Dutch, whose churches are conducting a very methodical anti-nuclear campaign — we know about the Roman Catholics of Poland — and in Australia, and throughout the world, we have the support of numbers of staunch rationalists.

Passive resistance is of course fraught with danger. (Gandhi referred to by the scientist-philosopher Albert Einstein as '...the only truly great figure of our age. Generations to come will scarcely believe that such a one as this ever walked this earth in flesh and blood...') Gandhi was assassinated in 1948. I personally feel that the dangers and suffering those who choose to practise passive resistance are bound to encounter are preferable to the moral seepage and contaminating ashes which will overwhelm those who passively accept the nuclear-holocaust their political leaders are preparing for them. Though I don't go along with President Reagan's practical suggestion, the aged are of less importance. I am old, childless. I've led a full life. You're the ones the issue concerns most deeply — the parents, the children, the grandchildren — the youth of the world — and particularly the youth of Australia, because Australia is ours, and you are the ones on whom this *potentially* great country depends. I know many of you young people have been badly done by in recent times. But my hope is that you will not let yourselves be ground down by despair — that you will rise above present social and economic injustices — that you will not hold *life* responsible for these — and that you will carry a banner into the kind of future we all want. One more point — if the powers were to see the light, halt the nuclear build up, and return to settling their differences by conventional means, we must remember that since the end of World War II nearly 40 million people have been killed by conventional weapons. So our work will not be done till we have eradicated the *habit* of war. But let it be understood — the battle we must win before all others is that of nuclear disarmament. However perilous the non-violent risks run by those who espouse this cause, I — and I hope, you too — would rather contribute to the *life* force than collaborate in the death of the world.

WHITE SHARED the platform with scientists from the USA and the USSR during a symposium in May at the Australian National University, Canberra where four hundred people discussed the threat and consequences of nuclear war.

A few months later, White's two plays *Netherwood* and *Signal Driver* were published.

Australians in a Nuclear War

1983

As an epigraph I'd like to quote from a poem by the Australian poet Robert Gray, *To the master Dōgen Zenji* (who lived from AD 1200-1253).

> He said, All that's important
> is the ordinary things.
>
> Making the fire
> to boil some bathwater, pounding rice, pulling the weeds
> and knocking dirt out of their roots,
>
> or pouring tea — those blown scarves,
> a moment, more beautiful than the drapery
> in paintings by a Master.
>
> — 'It is this world of the *dharmas*,
> (the atoms)
> which is the Diamond.'

For those who may be mystified, *dharma* is the Buddhist truth, the Hindu moral law; again the atoms are those small, ordinary things, as well as the truth, the Diamond being the acme of pure Truth. You will not find this irrelevant to what I have to say this morning.

I must say I groaned when invited to speak at this conference — like the friends and neighbours I bail up and ask, 'Are you going to take part in the anti-nuclear march?' In the last couple of years I've been doing this sort of thing constantly, often repeating myself, becoming an avoidable Doomsday bore. But anything of importance — like a garden, a human relationship, a child, a religious faith, even the most convinced brand of atheism has to be worked on constantly if it is to survive. So I agreed to speak this time round, and am starting off again to try to explain to my fellow Australians how to prepare themselves to face nuclear war. On this occasion my attempt is made far more difficult in that I am an amateur surrounded by experts in the sciences. But here goes. We are all in it together, and I expect many of my ordinary fellow Australians are as ignorant as I am of the developments of technology and the seemingly endless varieties of nuclear weapons.

My particular concern is how we may develop the *moral* strength, not so much to face as to call off the nuclear war with which the world is threatened. I feel it all starts with the question of identity. In recent years we have been served up a lot of claptrap about the need for a *national* identity. We have been urged to sing imbecile jingles, flex our muscles like the sportsmen from telly commercials, and display a hearty optimism totally unconvincing because so superficial and unnatural. Those who preach this doctrine are usually the kind of chauvinist who is preparing his country, not to avert war, but to engage in it. Anyhow, this is not the way to cultivate an Australian identity. For one thing, we are still in the melting pot, a rich but not yet blended stew of disparate nationalities. And most of us who were transplanted here generations ago, either willingly or unwillingly, the white overlords and their slave whites, are still too uncertain *in ourselves.* Australia will never acquire a national identity until enough *individual* Australians acquire identities of their own. It is a question of spiritual values and must come from within before it can convince and influence others. Then, when our individual identities, united in one aim, cluster together like a swarm of instinctively productive bees — as opposed to that other, coldly scientific, molecular cluster — we may succeed in achieving positive results.

But how to discover this personal identity? I'm always hearing remarks like, 'I feel insecure, I have no confidence.' When I tell them that I who have had everything one can expect from life in the way of recognition, awards, money and so forth, feel only intermittently secure and confident, many of those who hear me believe I am putting on an act, while others who had considered I am one who surely knows the answers, are depressed to find that, by my own admission, I don't. What I do know for certain is that what is regarded as success in a rational materialistic society only impresses superficial minds. It amounts to nothing and will not help us rout the destructive forces threatening us today. What may be our salvation is the discovery of the identity hidden deep in any one of us, and which may be found in even the most desperate individual, if he cares to search the spiritual womb which contains the embryo of what can be one's personal contribution to truth and life.

We must become aware of what Aldous Huxley refers to in his remarkable book *Ends and Means* as the 'existence of a spiritual reality underlying the phenomenal world and importing to it whatever value or significance it possesses'. Huxley saw the ethic of non-attachment as the means of attaining awareness of this spiritual reality, because the practice of non-attachment entails the practice of all the virtues — most important charity, but also that of courage, and the cultivation of intelligence, generosity, and disinterestedness.

The ideal of non-attachment has been preached again and again in the course of the last 3000 years. It is found in Hinduism, the teachings of Buddha, the doctrine of Lao Tsu, in the philosophy of the Greek Stoics. The Gospel of Jesus is essentially one of non-attachment to the things of this world, and of attachment to God. What the Jewish philosopher Spinoza calls 'blessedness' is simply the state of non-attachment, just as Spinoza's 'human bondage' is the condition of one who identifies himself with his own desires, emotions, and thought processes, or with their objects in the external world.

Again to quote Aldous Huxley, speaking from as far back as 1937, 'Closely associated with the regression in charity is the decline in men's regard for truth. At no period in the world's history has organized lying been practised so shamelessly, or, thanks to modern technology, so efficiently or on so vast a scale as by the political and economic dictators of the present century. Most of this organized lying takes the form of propaganda, inculcating hatred and vanity, and preparing men's minds for war. The principal aim of the liars is the eradication of charitable feelings and behaviour in the sphere of international politics. Technological advance is rapid, but without progress in charity, and awareness of the spiritual undertones and needs of everyday life, it is useless.'

What was true in 1937 is even more pertinent in 1983. Ironic that the age which invented the lie detector should now be using the sincerity machine. If he were alive today Huxley might be greatly amused at the predictability of human nature.

But to return to my own experience and the disappointment or disbelief of those who look to me for a lead. When I tell them I don't know the answers, I've got to admit I'm not being strictly truthful. I do, or I *have* known them, and shall again, but only intermittently, the result of a daily wrestling match, and then only by glimmers, as through a veil. None of the great truths can be more than half-grasped. I doubt I should have arrived anywhere near my inklings of them if it weren't for what I sense as links with a supernatural power.

Some of you will see it as a sign of reaction and weakness to introduce mysticism, perhaps even necromancy, into a situation where power politics and increasingly sophisticated technological resources would seem to be leading us inevitably towards nuclear war. However, because I've been asked to give some idea of how I think the Australian people might prepare themselves to face such a situation, I can only stick my neck out and offer my humble beliefs. If I become an outsider by doing so, this won't be a great hardship as I've been that as far back as I can remember — something strange and unacceptable in the eyes of those who believe they see straight. At least it's given me courage of a kind, which I'd like every Australian to acquire. I'd like them to rootle round in their unconscious and find this personal identity, the moral strength which is floating there amongst the trash — the filth. Oh yes, the trash is there in me too, otherwise I shouldn't be able to understand the violence which takes over in such events as bikie riots, the deliberate burning of forests, the destruction of schools — these and many other impulses which would contribute towards the act of violence we fear most.

So let each of us search for the good faith in us which may help save the world, even if we risk turning ourselves into outsiders in this materialistic, muscular Australian society. If we are to give consideration to this momentous issue we must go apart from time to time — apart from our families and friends — and they could think it very peculiar — our occasional evaporations, though we may be skulking only in the next room, or in a trance at the sink — till we find the courage and words to explain the reason for our behaviour — when perhaps we could find ourselves applauded by others who are contemplating similar action. For those who are still afraid of being seen as grotesque supporters of a lost cause, let them take notice of a human chain linked in protest throughout Britain and Europe, gathering resistance in the United States and nearer home the human river which recently flowed through the cynical streets of Sydney and down over the amphitheatre of the Domain, as in other capital cities of Australia. It's obvious we aren't alone.

Still, it is always dispiriting to come across the hordes of unconverted, as I did on my way to the anti-nuclear demo on 27 March — the thousands pouring into the Sydney Show and Sportsgrounds, and to wonder if anyone was aware of a cosmic threat. Did any of them give a passing thought to what might be done about it? Remembering that most human beings are conservative and tend to perform the actions that require least effort, to think the thoughts that are easiest, to feel the emotions that are most commonplace, to give rein to the desires that are most nearly animal, made the dilemma no easier to bear.

Most of these complacent souls have embraced the consumer religion. They have allowed the department store non-culture to persuade them that the accumulation of possessions — cars, TV sets, and unnecessary domestic appliances — is the sum of happiness. The craving for possessions and money, from the humble hire-purchase level, to the smash and grab tactics of the tirelessly acquisitive rich, from the alderman to the union leader and cabinet minister, and finally the dictator of a superpower, has become an epidemic disease. In such a climate, distrust grows between the man in the street and his neighbour. It can be a question of status, or simple paranoia, but more often it is justified by reality: the injustices of justice to which so many ordinary people are subjected. Over all, the suspicion that one nation has for another hatches the nuclear virus — the cause of our being here today in our various capacities.

Not so long ago a ray of light leapt at me out of the prevailing gloom. A series of historic incidents showed me that suspicion of one nation for another can be allayed if the head of one is brave or idealistic enough to take the lead and give his opponent reason for trust. I'm referring to an article by the American Professor Abraham Keller, President of Educators for Social Responsibilities, in which he points out that:

'On June 10, 1963, in a commencement address at the American University in Washington, President John Kennedy announced that the United States would no longer conduct bomb tests in the atmosphere. His speech was not only printed immediately in *Pravda,* but the *Voice of America* program which broadcast it was not jammed as its programs regularly were and the President's words quickly reached the Russian people. On June 11, in the United Nations, the Soviet Union withdrew its objections to a Western proposal to send observers to war-torn Yemen, a proposal it had been opposing as a capitalist plot. Three days later, on June 14, again at the United Nations, the United States withdrew its objection to the seating of the Hungarian delegation which it had been calling a puppet of the Soviet. The next day, June 15, President Kruschev took to the air congratulating Kennedy on his speech and announced that the Soviet Union was discontinuing the production of strategic bombers. In July the Soviet Union stopped its bomb tests in the atmosphere and on 5 August representatives of the two nations made the test ban final by signing the Treaty of Moscow, which was ratified by the United States Senate in September. On October 9 Kennedy lifted the grain embargo and allowed the shipment of 250-million dollars worth of wheat to the Soviet Union. Also in October the two nations signed a pact agreeing not to orbit nuclear weapons in space. Where years of negotiation for a test ban had failed, a single step by one of the partners brought brilliant success, and, though briefly, established a momentum of goodwill, which went beyond the bomb tests themselves. Then, in November 1963, John Kennedy was assassinated, and hopes for a continuation of the process which he had set in motion, and which had been received with exuberance by many, were buried with him.'

I don't know whether many of those Australians who write to the papers and see the Soviet as a permanent butt for vilification are aware of this exchange between the two major powers, but I would like them to take notice of Professor Keller's article as evidence that the Soviet, in spite of their brutal treatment of dissidents, the labour camps, and atrocities worthy of the Tsars they replaced, can respond to the civilised approach. Behind the Slav visor and the stereotype diplomatic suits there may even lurk a soul. How else could this barbarous nation have produced the poets Pushkin and Pasternak, the playwright Chekov, the novelists Tolstoy and Dostoevsky, and composers such as Moussorgsky, Tchaikovsky, Shostakovich and Stravinsky. (Incidentally, a backward glance at the barbarous and brutal shows that decent Australians contributed a fair measure of brutality in their treatment of convicts and Aborigines.)

To return to those writers of letters to the daily press, I'd like to quote one from a John McCrae of Balmain, Sydney, who seems to speak with authority instead of the hysteria discernible in many other outraged correspondents. 'In Communist countries peace marchers are shot', asserts one; to which McCrae replies, 'This is not so. On 1 August last year I was in Kiev, and on that day I saw a massive peace and disarmament rally through the city streets. On huge canvas placards suspended above and across the streets, were printed slogans in many foreign languages including English, advocating peace, and denouncing all forms of warfare. At the base of a nearby World War II memorial column, flowers surrounded it knee-deep, a tribute to the fallen.' The soil in which the seeds of truth and trust can be sown is there. It is to be found in the Communist state of East Germany, where a large demonstration was organized in Dresden to commemorate the 37th anniversary of the city's destruction by British and American bombers causing the deaths of 35,000 people — in East Germany where Bishop Hempel has proposed that the state should renounce the stationing of Soviet-built nuclear missiles in its territory, and has called for compulsory 'peace education' in East German schools.

I pray that the words spoken at this conference may carry beyond walls and reach thousands of ears hitherto deaf to warnings of the final catastrophe. I pray that we may convey to them the darkness of night which will fall upon the earth, the death of life in the oceans, the death of crops, trees, and herds, and the immediate or painful lingering death which will come to most of us. I pray that those who hear and see will join those other people of good will who are already working to avert disaster and that they will take heart from the positive results achieved by John Kennedy before his assassination.

Perhaps I can draw your attention to some other examples of non-violent revolution. No need by now to mention the achievements of Gandhi in South Africa and India. But many will be unaware that the Finns between 1901 and 1905 conducted a campaign of non-violent resistance to Russian oppression; this was completely successful and in 1905 the law imposing conscription on the Finns was repealed. Again, the long campaign of non-violent resistance conducted by the Hungarians under Deák was crowned with complete success in 1867. Deák refused political power and personal distinction, was unshakably a pacifist, and without shedding blood compelled the Austrian government to restore the Hungarian constitution. Deák succeeded where the ambitious, power-loving militarist Kóssuth had failed in 1848. In Germany, two campaigns of non-violent resistance were successfully carried out against Bismarck — the Kulturkampf by the Catholics, and the working-class campaign, after 1871, for recognition of the Social Democratic Party. More recently, non-violent resistance and non-co-operation were successfully used in modern Egypt against British domination. A striking example of the way in which even a threat of non-violent non-co-operation can avert war was provided by the British Labour Movement in 1920. The Council of Action formed that year warned the government that if it persisted in its scheme of sending British troops to Poland for an attack on the Russians, a general strike would be called, Labour would refuse to transport munitions or men, and a complete boycott of the war would be declared. Faced by this ultimatum, Lloyd George abandoned his plans for war.

History shows us repeatedly that non-violence can achieve positive results. But — again to quote Aldous Huxley:

'People prepare for war among other reasons because war is in the great tradition, because war is exciting and gives them certain personal and vicarious satisfaction, because their education has left them militaristically minded, because they live in a society where success, however achieved, is worshipped, and where competition seems more natural than co-operation. Hence the general reluctance to embark on constructive policies directed towards the removal at least of the economic causes of war. Hence, too, the extraordinary energy rulers and even the ruled put into such war-provoking policies as rearmament, the centralisation of executive power, and the regimentation of the masses.'

In Huxley's day, such policies were pursued by the great dictators Mussolini and Hitler. Very disturbing to many of us today is the way Thatcher fanned the emotions of the democratic British to fever pitch and led them into that lamentable swashbuckling expedition to the Falklands, to distract their attention from the state of affairs at home.

In the words of Mussolini, 'Fascism believes that war alone

brings up to its highest tension all human energy and puts the stamp of nobility upon the peoples who have the courage to meet it.' Surely the same sentiments were belted out loud and clear in Thatcher's tirades at the time of the Falklands campaign.

Of course torrents of water have flooded under the bridge since the illuminating months which preceded John Kennedy's assassination, waters which haven't carried us forward, but sucked us back to where we were. The aged cowboy filmstar Ronald Reagan has called upon the scientific community who gave us nuclear weapons to turn their great talents to the cause of mankind and world peace — to give us the means of rendering these nuclear weapons impotent and obsolete. The chief source of stimulus to the fantasies in President Reagan's Reader's-Digest mind is the diabolical Edward Teller, so-called 'Father of the H-Bomb' who is still around at the age of 75. I shall leave Teller's latest nuclear tricks to the experts, confining myself to mention of his obsession that the Russians are totally evil, totally cunning. Nobody is that. I can recognise a certain amount of evil in myself, for instance, but would lay claim to a little good. So with all of us: there is material to work on.

However, I cannot prevent myself suspecting that those who devised the comparatively primitive bombs which were dropped on Hiroshima and Nagasaki, and who have since gone on to develop more sophisticated nuclear weapons, are totally evil. I don't think I am ghoulish in saying that I would like them, and every morally responsible citizen of the world, particularly my fellow Australians of the World War II period, to refresh their memories by referring regularly to the photographic record of the Hiroshima-Nagasaki happening — the rags of human flesh, the suppurating sores, the despair of families blown apart, the disturbed minds, the bleak black gritty plains where the homes of human beings like you and me once stood. Most of all, I would like every Australian *couple* born since Hiroshima and Nagasaki were blasted out of existence to consult these photographic records and for ever after do all in their power to prevent the children they are creating from suffering a fate similar to that thrust upon the children of those two Japanese cities. Let us rouse ourselves and realise this is what we shall have to face. Australians are not prepared for anguish. I don't mean only in the sense of personal bereavement, but in the true spiritual sense, when we feel that God may have forsaken the world, the God many of us probably won't have given a thought to, until the crunch comes in a cosmic flash. Either we are exterminated completely, or worse, we linger on — the rags of flesh, the sores, the disturbed mind. If we are to bear this at all, it will be through God's grace, by cultivating human dignity, and by our ability to dispense with the superfluous details of life as we have known it.

I look to the women of this world, who are in many cases more perceptive than the men and possessed of a determined physical and moral strength — witness the women of Britain and their opposition to Cruise missiles.

The other day I came across an aphorism from Rudyard Kipling's *Plain Tales from the Hills.* Not my favourite writer — too much the imperialist bully of his period — but in this little aphorism he reveals a curiously perceptive, *feminine* sensitivity. Listen to it: *A woman's guess is much more accurate that a man's certainty.* From my childhood onward I have felt this particularly in Australia, and contemporary Australian women could play a leading part in preparing us to face and avert nuclear warfare, where all is uncertain, and where the masculine mind may be too orthodox in its approach. I hope I am not castrating anybody by making this remark. I am speaking of women of the stuff from which the early feminists were recruited, before they were persuaded to see themselves as female eunuchs, and surrender much of their strength. As for the male animal, I see him as strengthened by recognising the feminine element in his psyche. The Australian male has shown himself unquestionably courageous in facing up to dangers and death in a series of conventional wars. But the dangers and death we shall have to face in a nuclear war are of a somewhat different order. The fact that the death of a planet may occur raises the issue from a humanist to an eschatological level — spiritual as well as material death, involving judgment, heaven, and hell; though personally I can't go along with the theological concept of hell. For me, hell is here on earth, living in the shadow of the giant mushroom, with maniacs like Reagan and Teller calling the tune.

That our fate is not entirely in their hands is due to the fact that the people of the world are stirring, finding a voice — enlightened scientists aware of the folly of a war neither side can win — medical men who will bear the brunt of a nuclear disaster without the means for coping with it — high-rank Army officers who have been through other wars and seen the light — economists and sociologists appalled by the billions poured into the manufacture of arms instead of into the bellies of the hungry — churchmen at last recognising their former hierarchic pride and capitalist ambitions. Most encouraging is the stand made by the Roman Catholic bishops of the United States — the Archbishop of Canterbury in Thatcher's dehumanized Britain — and the British Council of Churches, an interdenominational Protestant organisation which, in a recent debate on the nuclear arms race, passed a resolution: 'There are circumstances in which Christian obedience demands civil *dis*-obedience.'

A long course of evil-doing can result in all concerned becoming so sick of destruction and degeneration that they decide to change their ways, thus transforming evil into good. I like to think that the anti-nuclear movement throughout the world is proof that this has begun to happen.

Leaders of the world community have set us a heartening example. How then, can we, the ordinary folk who have no specific role to play, contribute? I include myself in this category because I have no position or skill which might prevent a showdown or alleviate the suffering caused by what we may fail to avert. I am one of you millions of *beings*. Being in itself can be a contribution if it is a concerned being, if we are prepared to offer our *selves* as a sacrifice — that murmurous cluster of human bees I mentioned earlier — a mass sacrifice in the cause of non-violence and the continuance of life on earth.

Curiously, when the fortress of misguided values is occupied by the likes of Reagan and Teller (even members of the British Royal Family have joined the enemy by publicly advocating nuclear deterrents) I have derived immense comfort, hope, faith, inspiration from a great American, the Cistercian monk-teacher-activist Thomas Merton. Initially a contemplative religious, Merton's spiritual drive was aimed at halting the dehumanization of man in contemporary society, a sickness he saw as leading to mass violence and ultimately nuclear war. War of any kind is abhorrent. Remember that since the end of World War II, over 40 million people have been killed by conventional weapons. So, if we should succeed in averting nuclear war, we must not let ourselves be sold the alternative of conventional weapons for killing our fellow men. We must cure ourselves of the habit of war. Or is this too fanciful an aim? However the sceptics may shrug, I shall continue to preach non-violence to all those who face the contingency of nuclear or any kind of war, and hope that my fellow Australians, from reading and hearing about murder, rape, arson, petty theft and condoned embezzlement in their everyday life, in this so-called 'pure' country, will not have become so callous that they ignore the greatest opportunity for unity which history has offered the nations of the world. This I see as the positive side of the the nuclear threat. The spirit may triumph where politics (the League and the United Nations), socio-political faiths such as Marxism, Italian Fascism and German National-Socialism — all have failed. I see our only hope in faith, charity, and in humbling ourselves before man and God.

In the 14th Century an anonymous English mystic wrote a book called *The Cloud of Unknowing*, the main theme of which is that God cannot be apprehended by man's intellect and that only love can pierce the 'cloud of unknowing' which lies between Him and us. I feel that in my own life anything I have done of possible worth has happened in spite of my gross, worldly self. I have been no more than the vessel used to convey ideas above my intellectual capacities. When people praise passages I have written, more often than not I can genuinely say, 'Did I write that?' I don't think this is due to my having a bad memory, because I have almost total recall of trivialities. I see it as evidence of the part the supernatural plays in lives which would otherwise remain earthbound.

It occured to me in a recent re-reading of *The Cloud of Unknowing* and through my discovery of Tom Merton's works that there may be a connection between the cloud in which God's wisdom is hidden from the human intellect and that other cloud which has never dispersed from above Hiroshima and Nagasaki. It could be that this satanical mushroom, preserved by photographic plates and human memory, is given us as an icon, or reminder that we contain the seeds of evil and destruction as well as the seeds of divine regeneration. Time is running out. In 1983 it is up to us to choose which we are going to cultivate.

CITIZENS FOR DEMOCRACY, filled with spirited optimism, called a meeting in Sydney on 11 November to plan a series of People's Conventions all around Australia to agitate for a new constitution in 1988 — the year of the Bicentenary. White spoke, together with the then Deputy Prime Minister Lionel Bowen and the then Attorney-General Gareth Evans. It was at this meeting that he accepted his nomination as Republican of the Year.

A New Constitution

1983

I'M GOING to be brief tonight, because tomorrow I set out on a long journey, and having spoken to you on other commemorative occasions I don't want to bore people by repeating myself. However, as you've asked me to run this risk, I'll stick my neck out and recall how on 11 November eight years ago I had invited a few friends to dinner to honour the late David Campbell, one of our greatest poets. I was plodding away drearily cooking the meal, when I turned on the radio for company, and became part of a real nightmare. In Canberra, one of the most extraordinary events in Australian history was taking place — the dismissal of Gough Whitlam and the elected Government by the Governor General, Sir John Kerr, and the Archconspirator, Malcolm Fraser. I was as stunned as those whose voices came pouring into my kitchen from the steps of Parliament House. The sauce I was stirring curdled. My guests began arriving. We were all stunned. During dinner we kept the radio playing, hoping for some glimpse of reason. But it didn't come.

Over the years that evening has remained vivid in my memory — as it has, I'm sure in the memory of anyone who looks for honesty in human behaviour. That includes many of those who supported the Archconspirator politically. They have remained mortified; otherwise they would not have continued supporting Citizens For Democracy, trying to ensure, along with all of us, that nothing like it should occur again.

I have to confess I'm here on this platform tonight under false pretences. I can't claim to be an expert on constitutional change and must leave it to those among you who are. I only know I want this change, to protect our evolving nation from anything similar to the Whitlam dismissal happening to it in the future.

Though a member of an English family which came to Australia from Somerset in 1826 I must say the British Monarchy means less and less to me as time passes. How much less must it mean to Greeks, Italians, Spaniards, Chinese, and all those other nationalities of which Australia is now composed? Particularly the Greeks, natural republicans, whose unnatural monarchy was foisted on them by the Great Powers. Unnatural monarchies were in fact strung across Europe — from Italy, through Yugoslavia, Greece, Bulgaria, Romania — countries which managed to divest themselves of these parasitic clusters in the latter part of our century.

Monarchies seem better adapted to a temperate climate — Scandinavia — Holland — and 'Home', it goes without saying. (My parents encouraged travel only in these decent, 'white' countries, never in the 'black', passionate South.) Of the surviving monarchies only the British continues to proliferate — children, cousins, the cousins of cousins — till branches of the vine overflow the Palace balcony when on display for loyal subjects. We can hardly object. Let the subjects revel in their loyalty, and dressmakers and milliners enjoy the advantages which come of royal patronage.

But what does this do for me — the colonial boy — and the aforementioned Austral-Greeks, -Italians, -Chinese and so forth? Admittedly some of the *grand* Austral-Greeks etc. will feel their money safer if they can snuggle up under Big British Mummy's umbrella. But most of the hard-bitten Scots I know, and Irish whose forebears were shipped out to New South Wales, however trivial the sins they had committed, pay only cynical homage to the Crown. (I do not include the Queen of England's Irish knight, who obviously felt a need in his Ascendancy soul when clawing at her son's arm for the recognition he received. Or perhaps Sir Neddy* is a cynic too.)

I believe most of the Democratic Citizens throughout Australia don't even know they are till some crisis, brought on usually by the elements, humbles them into classlessness. It might be by touching a red-hot half-empty iron tank, by sharing with other parched throats the warm sludge at the bottom of a canvas water-bag, by contemplating the charred remains of a house they had built, or supporting one another amongst the wreckage caused by a still active hurricane. At such times humanity replaces politics. We become ordinary democratic Australians.

Not a monarchist, I must say I took to Princess Anne on her recent visit, an outsider in her family like myself in mine. I enjoyed her dismissal of the *Women' Weekly* mentality which keeps the monarchy going in this country — her admission that she hadn't read much that is Australian, though she'd seen the *Women's Weekly* occasionally. 'Didn't she like it?' a loyal subject asked; 'it's so Australian'. Her reply, 'Poor you'.

Poor us, in many ways — in spite of the bulldust we spray around to distract our attention from reality. I am old now. At least I hope I can stave off senility and death till a few of my ambitions are realised: that I can see justice done by the Aborigines, in retribution for some of the infamies of the past, *and* the present — and justice for those of any colour who exist not much above starvation. *Justice* — not just a cynical theory — obedience to the *letter* of the law — which is what seems to prevail in a society where pretentiousness, greed, and corruption are rife. Let me see the day when Australians in high places no longer ape the brash flash image, or accept the policies of our temporary masters, the Yanks. I pray for the day when we are independent of any other nation. Let me be around when the Australian Republic is proclaimed so that I can fly the Eureka flag above my garden. Whatever the dangers we may have to face in the future, let us face them honourably, and as ourselves.

INVITED by the democratic Greek Government to celebrate the fall of the military junta, White travelled to Athens in November intending to give this speech. But in the festive excitement it was never actually delivered.

Greece — My Other Country

1983

I HAD resigned myself to not seeing Greece again. Age and its ailments make it an undertaking to fly from one *Australian* capital to another, let alone from *our* hemisphere to yours. So I had refused tempting offers from Canada and Britain. Now I have probably offended two distinguished universities by accepting the Greek Government's invitation to take part in your commemoration. How could I resist returning at this point, when the close ties of love and friendship, the events of history, and those vertiginous landscapes of yours, tell me that Greece is my other country? Not that I haven't been frequently disgusted by some of its material aspects, as those who have read my books will know. But these depressing details of the Greek experience only serve to bring Greece closer, make it more recognisably part of my own flawed self. Anyhow, here I am amongst you today.

I came first to Greece at the end of the German Occupation. I started to learn about you from Egypt — studying maps — making my first attempts at your exacting language. My face was turned this way throughout Hitler's War — from Alexandria, the Western Desert, Cyrenaica, Palestine, and Cyprus. I had admired Greek courage from the moment when your answer to the Italians was NO, and again when you and our Australian troops stood side by side in the Cretan campaign and you ran great risks in covering our withdrawal.

After the German occupation, a year spent outside Athens with the RAF, helping train Greek pilots in operational intelligence, increased my knowledge and love of Greece. I formed a number of friendships which have lasted ever since. As life seeped back into the bullet-scarred Athens its citizens were more joyous than I have known them in better times. There was singing in the streets. Food began to reappear in the tavernas. The smell of those days remains with me — the perfume of stocks in the Maroussi fields, chestnuts roasting at street corners, Kokkoretsi turning on spits in open doorways. And the roses, the crimson roses...

As one who has always been stage-struck, I spent my evenings when on leave at the theatre — seeing Kotopouli in the last years of her career, and your Minister for Culture, then a little girl, playing the ingénue in an English piece with Katerina's company. I saw Miranda, who rode the white horse at the Battle of Kephissia, and later took the part of Theodora in the play about that empress by Dimitri Photiadis. The frivolous side of my nature rejoiced particularly in the popular theatre, those mercilessly satirical revues, with stars such as the Sisters Kalouta, Kakia Mendri, Hero Handa, and the Vempo (first seen in Beirut when that city was a haven of peace and beauty.)

Memorable years. At times I forgot which country should have come first, and fell foul of my Commanding Officer for sympathising with the KKE.

My departure from Greece was a stormy one as we rounded Capes Malea and Teneron, heading for Italy and the train journey across a frozen Europe for demobilisation in London. I returned to Australia and decided to re-settle there. It was not easy to re-adjust to the country of my origin. The years which followed were unhappy ones. I was not accepted as a writer, nor as an Australian, and was said to be posing as a member of my own family. Xenophobia was rife in those days.

Then I started returning to Greece with my friend of over 40 years, Manoly Lascaris. We travelled the country from the pine forests of Florina to the Mani's gnarled claw. We landed on practically every island worthy of the name. Again we smelled Egypt and North Africa standing on a dusty ledge on Santorini. We made our pilgrimage to the Holy Mountain and the Polis, then past Nicaea down to Smyrna escaping at last with relief to Chios in a little vessel called 'Aphrodite.'

A later visit coincided with the era of the torturers, whose fall we are celebrating today. Life had gone out of the Greece we knew. Some of our friends, among them Manoly's brother-in-law Dimitri Photiadis, had been banished to Aegean rocks. Fascist posters plastered Metsovo, and were strung across the streets of villages in Pelion, where the century before the painter Theophilos recorded the Turkish occupation and your War of Independence.

The Greek soul was born of foreign occupation — Turkish, German, British, American. In Australia our experience of foreign occupation is growing. The American bases are a sinister warning; in its different way, infiltration by Japanese business; and we are scarcely ever without members of the British Royal Family. Evidence of Oz police brutality is strangely reminiscent of tactics in the days of the Junta. It is time we, like you, cherish our independence — especially since Kissinger recently came among us to snare those who are ripe for seduction.

Australia has not yet suffered as you have, but whatever Greece has endured in the past is nothing to the concert of suffering she may be called on to share with the rest of Europe, even with ourselves in our remote island-continent — the fate which is being prepared for us by the feckless American cowboy and his advisers, the power-hungry British Boadicea, and the faceless Russian — the nuclear war which could destroy the world.

This time we are *all* in it. Never have the people of the world been threatened to such an extent by the power of their leaders. And never have the people united as they are uniting now in the face of danger. Because — with due respect to some of those we know — we have lost faith in politicians and diplomacy. Intent on remaining in office and the juggling act of keeping a number of admittedly important issues in the air at once, they cannot concentrate on what so many of us see as the blinding issue of the century.

Now the powerless realise they must exercise their power

— the youth, the poets, churchmen, doctors — the *women*. When I specify women I'm not speaking so much of the aggressive feminists and intellectual theorists, as the ordinary wives and mothers who keep an eye on the soup, who go out foraging for the weeds during occupation by foreign armies, and who, as some I know, have experienced the most real and personal pain, giving birth to children, in blood and sweat, in the street and on the kitchen table. These are the women who will understand what I'm saying, and who are now responding throughout the world.

It may seem inappropriate to raise the spectre of nuclear war in the midst of your celebrations. I can't agree. It is a possibility we must never allow ourselves to lose sight of. You Greeks gave the world civilisation. Since the fall of Byzantium it has been preserved by the Panayia and the Saints — as you know in your hearts, even those of you who *profess* not to 'believe'. Surely we must not allow the barbarians of today to destroy by holocaust this civilisation you have created? Apathy and ignorance persuade a lot of my countrymen to turn their backs on an event so monstrous it could carry off in a flash everything we take for granted, the necessary utensils of our daily lives, together with our families and homes, as happened in many cases when those *primitive* atomic bombs were dropped on the inhabitants of Hiroshima and Nagasaki. Better to go in a flash, perhaps, like those who disappeared during that trial run — than to linger with death in our blood — in the aftermath of nuclear war on a grand scale — a lingering which scientists believe humankind will share with forests, pastures, crops, flocks and herds, and life in the oceans. I would ask you Greeks, who are amongst the world's greatest survivors, to meditate on this theme when your celebrations are over, and to unite with those other people of the world — ordinary people — who stand for *life* as opposed to the arbitrary death the super-powers wish upon our planet.

THIS article was written for Australia Day and published in the *Sydney Morning Herald*. It drew a flood of Letters to the Editor. Some described it as 'spiteful' and 'childish', 'verbal sludge' by 'an intellectual bigot'; others read it as 'courageous', 'compassionate', and 'astute observation' by 'one of the most forward minds of our time'.

Patriotism

1984

SOME YEARS ago I went to a performance of Louis Nowra's *Inside the Island* and wrote my opinion of it to the press when, to my mind, a leading critic dismissed it unreasonably. Meeting the critic eventually, I was told, 'You only like that play because it rubbishes Australia'.

My reply was, 'It appealed to me because it rubbishes a lot of the rubbish in Australia' — in fact, dusty colonial traditions and a conservative mentality which aims at having us huddle for ever under Big Mummy's Edwardian parasol.

Looking back at 'patriotism' as I have seen it displayed by Australians, I can remember it in my childhood at the end of World War I as an orgy of flag wagging and processions of returning soldiers. During the war there were moments of intense personal grief, understandable even to my child's mind when news of individual deaths was received by those I loved. German neighbours were pelted with rotten vegetables and fruit. Dachshunds were stoned. Later came the visit of the Prince of Wales (afterwards Edward VIII). The English Prince Charming drove through the city in a motorcade. There were the inevitable fireworks, crushes on the prince, ladies dropping curtseys, and embalming the glove he had shaken. To a child member of an Anglophile family it all seemed natural enough. I enjoyed wearing a little pin with three ostrich feathers and the motto *Ich Dien*. In 1983, much the same rituals erupted with the visit of the present Prince of Wales, his clotheshorse waxwork of a wife and their firstborn — the wives of plutocrats, bureaucrats, and subscribers to

women's magazines falling over one another to drop their curtseys, and whirl in the dance at a J. C. Williamson ball.

During World War II I did not witness Australia's patriotic
reactions. I saw something of the Blitz on London and served
with the RAF in the Middle East. In spite of their monarchy,
that great stimulus to British loyalty, patriotism was rather
muted when bombs began falling on Britain. In the Middle
East repeated advance and retreat to and fro across the desert
had its moments of stirring heroism as opposed to patriotic
heroics. In many of these operations Australian and other
Commonwealth troops took part.

On one occasion the Duke of Gloucester visited an air force
wing to which I belonged. He appeared a bored and boring
man straight out of an Edwardian Teutonic print. With his
glazed blue eyes and high-pitched voice he looked and
sounded a joke to most of us.

During my stay with the wing some kind of celebratory
dinner was held in the mess. My English commanding officer
announced I must propose the toast to the Crown. I asked
him if he knew I was a republican. He ordered me to do as
told: wasn't he my CO? So I gave him his toast well laced with
irony. Not long after, I was posted elsewhere, to the relief of
both of us.

Back in Australia after Hitler's War I was alienated by the
spectacle of a Prime Minister weaving romantic fantasies
round a Queen he hoped would remain a symbol for the class
he represented. From a distance I experienced the nightmare
of Vietnam created by those who saw us as servants of the
United States. For Australian patriotism changes its complex-
ion, or is changed willy-nilly from decade to decade without
our so far acquiring a firm identity of our own.

Over the years I have learnt to appreciate the worth of
simple Australians who sincerely love their country, though
in recent times this love is deflected into wrong channels by
politicians and manipulators of moral values, jingle writers,
the eternal flag waggers and sports promoters. It seems as
though life itself now depends on sport, with a Prime Minister
who materialises miraculously as cheer-leader at every sport-

ing event. This would be less nauseating if it could be seen as genuinely patriotic rather than political. But vote-catching, alas, lurks behind most moves on the politician's chessboard, and the capitalist's beady eye fossicks after more money, not so much for the good of the economy as his own aggrandisement. Too many Australians put their pockets before their country.

Money — one of the curses of life from century to century, breeding war, despair in the poor, dishonesty in the ambitious, while the hungry are encouraged to believe they will eat if they go along with what is planned for them. Look at the undernourished in Australia today as prices go up in the supermarket and politicians and the professional classes thrive. Drop eggs into a bowl of water and the bad ones swim to the top. So with human beings, the true are more often than not submerged, the specious rise.

Rummaging in garbage bins among the lobster and oyster shells and steak trimmings of the wealthy, can the hungry be expected to accept economic theory and come up meekly with patriotism? Do the politicians for whom they have voted really imagine the humble pensioner will continue to accept leaders who grab for more while their own miserable allowance for a cuppa and a slice of bread is cut?

Sweat-shirts on children and the roar of the crowds as we swipe the visiting team have no connection with patriotism, but this is genuinely alive in many who have sweated through drought and fire over the years and learnt to love their country the hard way.

As we embark on 1984, those with genuine love of their heritage have begun to wonder whether nationalism, in its overheated fuzz of artificially inseminated patriotism, is all that desirable. Should we thump our own tub when the human race is threatened with extinction? Isn't it more important to join with other concerned groups, regardless of nationality, class, politics, profession, or sex, in attempting to control the super powers and their satellites, and to remind our own leaders constantly of their election promises, as the itch to turn uranium into gold, edges them closer to selling out on humanity?

During World War II in the Western Desert of Egypt, I was obsessed by memories of the Australian landscape. The landscape became for me the Land, images round which my own patriotism formed more positively: frosty mornings on the Monaro, with sulphur-crested cockatoos toppling the stooked oats; floodwaters of the Barwon and Namoi through which I swam my horse to fetch the mail; the peppertrees and cracked asphalt of steamy Sydney streets. After returning to Australia, to live for ever after it seems, I went through a phase of apathy, revived hope under the idealist reformer and champion of the masses, followed by disillusion when the cold schemer took possession in the name of self-interest (or should we give him the benefit of his final burst of tears?)

Today, with nuclear war hanging over an Australia composed of so many nationalities, it is impossible not to see us as a microcosm of the world it is our duty to help protect. Australia will not be excluded from the train of events, and I find it unbearable to visualise our towering anthill cities reduced to rubble, at the cost of so many innocent ant lives.

If our patriotism is to be of any worth it must be twin-faceted, reflecting allegiance to Australia and the world. At the same time I feel we must beware of such sentimental, political, and material ties of the past, as those with the British monarchy, the CIA, Japanese business, silly flirtations with the Soviet Union for individual gain, and lately the Kissinger connection. We shall flounder of course in our attempts to evolve, and I shall be ridiculed as an idealist, an anarchist, a lunatic. Hedonistic Australians must be prepared to suffer — for we shall in any event.

Look at Greece — a truly patriotic nation. Ever since their War of Independence when they threw off the Turk, then occupation by various foreign powers, the monarchies forced on them by nations greater than their own, and from which they have had to divest themselves, the Greeks have suffered, and risen above their suffering.

I believe Australia, the untried, must be prepared to face the same fate sooner or later. The wars we have taken part in have not been fought on our own soil. How are we preparing for the future? Sport is not enough. Sportsmen are unsportsmanlike prima donnas, so often venal. The exposure of dishonesty in politicians, lawyers, doctors, trade union leaders is not unusual. There are many noble exceptions, of course. But when accepted or shrugged off, the lies and chicanery, the moral crimes committed by important members of society are passed on like contagious diseases through every level of the community. If blood, to borrow from Henry Lawson, has not yet stained the wattle, her roots, you might say, are in the sewer. When the moral standards of so many of us are rotted, how can we renew ourselves and join humankind in facing the greatest test of all?

We must search our hearts.

IN MARCH White again visited the Australian National University, Canberra. This time to launch the book *Australia and Nuclear War* containing papers, including his own, given at the anti-war symposium held there in May the previous year.

From Wigan to Wagga

1984

WHEN I was asked to come here and launch this important book, I was to say the least, diffident. I'm neither a scientist, nor a historian — nor am I a professional launcher, if that is the term. In fact, the only book I ever launched was one of Manning's Many Volumes, in this same city. In that instance, friendship and Australia made me knuckle under. In this, I feel I owe it to all those dedicated men and women who gathered here last year to discuss nuclear war, nuclear disarmament, and to oppose the superpowers who are planning what could be the death of life on earth.

War of any kind is abhorrent, as those who have taken part in one should know. It amazes me that anyone who has, can envisage another. But the organisers of a war are most of them excused from taking part. Look back at the horse-and-buggy days of World War I. I shall quote a passage from that extraordinary writer William Gerhardie describing the attitude of some of the more important members of British Society at the time. Some of these favoured 'persons', says Gerhardie, 'paid their visits to the Western Front to see the sights. Margot Asquith came, lodged with the King and Queen of the Belgians, ran up and stood excitedly on the top of a hillock, and exchanged cigarettes for a Belgian soldier's cartridge belt and lanyard. Dear Arthur came (Arthur being Balfour), gazed wonderously through his pince-nez at the shells bursting in the distance, remarking on their aesthetic aspect. Curzon came, expressing casually his incredulity as he observed some Tommies bathing in a pool, that the lower orders should look almost exactly like ourselves.' What Gerhardie describes was admittedly at the beginning, before the fields of Belgium and France were reduced to mud, their woods to tree-skeletons, and a generation of men laid lifeless in the earth.

But so it goes: the same, but different.

Twenty-one years later, the curtain went up on ACT II: Hitler's hordes spilling over Europe, bombs falling on Britain, the children evacuated from London. The difference between Wars I and II was that most of us were in the second, only the smart and the wealthy were in a position to take refuge in New York or resume their bridge in comfortable hotels in the remoter parts of Scotland. But any who remained could make contact with the bomb on which their names were written.

If at this point I come out with a grisly little anecdote, it isn't to be deliberately tasteless or to curdle your blood. It's that such anecdotes can bring home the personal side of the tragi-farce war can become for anyone experiencing it. During the Blitz on London I came across a Cockney charwoman who had worked for me in the days of peace. Now she was looking pale and exhausted. After a particularly gruelling night in the suburb where she lived, she had gone in search of a friend whose street had become a stretch of rubble along which a search was in progress — when the warden in charge of operations suddenly held up a head, and asked, 'Anyone know the body that belonged to this?' 'And,' my Mrs Collins told in her dusty Cockney, 'it was my friend's.'

Only a vignette — Mrs Collins and her friend's severed head in their London slum — or a charred tank in the Libyan desert, a crew member caught by the ankle as he tried vainly to escape from its burning hulk, — or a Cretan woman gunned almost in two by allied soldiers who claimed she had given one of their mates a dose of VD — all minor details illustrating the gratuitous brutality an individual can be subject to, inside the pattern of a war vast enough to include European Jewry slaughtered in their ghettos or carted off to the gas chambers, the wrecking of noble cities like Coventry and Dresden, and of course the apocalyptic end to World War II with the disappearance of Hiroshima and Nagasaki in fire, ashes, and agony such as mankind probably never experienced before.

And now we must face the possibility that a third act is being prepared. Hence the publication of this book, put together out of the research, the discussion, and findings of the men and women assembled at this university last year from Europe, the United States, and Australia. I don't think anyone could dispute the sincerity of the investigators, or fail to be impressed by the area covered. If some of the arguments are intuitive and emotional, that too, is good. For the hard bones of reason can be more powerful when fleshed out with feminine virtues. Thus fortified, we should be better able to prepare for the cataclysm, and, one hopes, avert it.

How can anyone who lived through World War II, if only on its fringes, prepare to organise the decimation of humanity? Except that the planners are the same worshippers of power and money, obsessed by ideologies. Nature, human beings, are of lesser importance.

Human beings...Aren't we the same more or less warped souls, the same imperfect compound of flesh and blood stumbling between progress and backsliding? Consider the photographs most of you must have seen published recently in our press — the Andropov family grieving for the Russian leader. As a family grotesque, compared with most families in the West, but their grief not unlike that which can rack any stay-at-home family from Winnipeg to Wichita, from Wigan to Wagga. Look also at a recent photograph of the Reagans as they sip their *ritual* orange juice, beautifully posed in profile by the traditional Hollywood PR expert. Perhaps they appear more human than the Andropovs, anyway to consumer eyes. At least the Russians have experienced the ravaging of their Russian soil. What, I wonder, does the Cowboy know about wargames, unless on celluloid, or from military reports and scientific drawing boards?

Take Thatcher. She must know something of war from the Battle of Britain. In spite of the strident patriotism, her conscience must have been stricken by the dead during her first, humiliating, and fairly bloody fling as Britannia hell-bent in the Falklands Campaign. Can she summon up humility enough to play the mediator after the visit to Moscow? As a woman she might if her woman's subtlety is not consumed by her vanity and brash vulgarity. Her insensitivity to the plight of the British working classes, and her determination to see nuclear missiles installed on British soil hardly reassure.

There is hope for us all, however, as this book will show; I would like to see copies of it flown to all major countries. There is hope in the efforts of the world's concerned scientists, doctors, churchmen, determined women, and thoughtful ordinary people in their increasing numbers, beaverlike behind the glittery confusion of high level talks, working breakfasts, and banquets, not forgetting the numbers game so dear to Australian politicians, and the itch which possesses some of them in the name of *morality,* to sell uranium to those who could become dealers in death.

Fortunately, millions of us have memories of the days when Hiroshima and Nagasaki were rubbed out by the first atomic bombs put to military use. We must keep these images of desolation constantly in mind, and hold them up as a warning to our youth. Resistance and survival will also depend on love — the love of those closely related to the physical and spiritual realities of whichever land they inhabit. Megaton piled on megaton of explosive power will achieve nothing — *literally* nothing, however the advocates of nuclear war on either side may try to delude themselves. Finally, I shall repeat a suggestion I have already made: I believe that those of us who are not actively in league with the powers of darkness — in other words, the majority of the world's population — could find the peace we long for, through greater understanding of the similarities and differences in human nature.

Thank you for listening to what I've had to say about — *our* book — *your* book — *THE* BOOK.

On 2 AUGUST White delivered the last in a series of lunchtime lectures to students and staff at La Trobe University, Melbourne on the theme *The Search for an Alternative to Futility*.

His scathing attacks on Prime Minister Bob Hawke and the ALP were picked up by the media. In this speech White claimed that his advice to Hawke had been ignored because he was 'from the brotherhood of untouchables, otherwise poofs'. Three weeks later on Channel 9 Hawke responded by describing White's position as being 'the most intellectually untenable and indeed reprehensible intervention I can recall'.

In this World of Hypocrisy and Cynicism

1984

FRIENDS — possibly a few Enemies too.

When I was asked some time ago if I would speak at La Trobe on the theme, *The Search for an Alternative to Futility,* I hesitated, though most of my later life, my daily occupation has been a search, without finding satisfactory answers. So many people demand answers that can't be refuted —not realising this is impossible if the issue is a transcendent one — when the search itself remains the important part. So I continued hesitating, particularly as I became more depressed by the way things are going in Australia and the world and it seemed futile to expect the lifting of despair. Then I felt I must pull myself together. I was letting down so many people — ordinary people whose positive attitudes must be consolidated. When I say 'ordinary' I am falling for a *cliché* — because so many of you who are considered ordinary — anonymous — are the extraordinary people we depend on to save the world in these days of political cynicism and dishonesty. We can no longer depend on our leaders anywhere on this threatened planet. This wonderful earth! Every morning as I stumble round the park across from the house where I live, dragged by my large, insistent dog, through frost, fog, bird calls, a sun rising through watered cloud, or later in the year, from behind solid dollops of ice-cream cumulus, to the clash of brass, the tinkle of humidity, I am strengthened by the natural phenomena I see around me. My eye is rejoiced by the texture of brick in a slum wall. Reasons for hope can even be found in those brief breathing spaces of a great city, those pocket handkerchiefs of grass littered with fragments of broken glass and the vomit from victims of the society in which we live.

I suppose such reflexions make me a sentimentalist in these days of *pragmatism*. I wonder what the promoters of this frayed term understand it to mean? Does it refer to reality? I would like to know what they, in their blindness, *see* as reality — the politicians in their politician suits, their background of law degrees, and air of dubious authority. Lawyers, dealing with human beings every day of their lives, act within a theory of life — the Law. Twice divorced from life, first by law, then through politics, the politician has about him an added pathos. Even those of them who have come up the hard way have lost contact with today's supermarket and the simple needs of the average human being, while making pronouncements on the *economy* — another of those myths. I shall go so far as to call it a lie.

In this world of hypocrisy and cynicism, hunger and despair, more and more people are relating to their own conception of reality. I expect some of those listening to me will be prepared to accuse me too, of hypocrisy and cynicism, coming as I do from a moneyed Australian family. But I must defend the unfortunate parents who sponsored this cuckoo. They were people of great principle from whom, if it is any consolation to them, I like to think my own, different priniples evolved. I remember from my childhood, at the end of World War I, my parents forcing on their friends a book with the title *Honour or Dollars*. Who wrote it I can't remember today, when I am following in their footsteps, hawking round what I consider an important book *The Forgotten Treaties* with, I suspect, as little success as Mum and Dad experienced then. Curious genes and history repeat themselves!

What I am about to tell you is not to give myself a pat on the back, but to show that you can't do much on your own. We must unite — those of us of similar vision in Australia and throughout the world — those of us who have lost faith in leaders. Some time ago I started sending copies of *The Forgotten Treaties* to members of our cabinet and some of the more important union men. To each of them I wrote — not a circular letter — but a personal message appealing to the man I thought each to be. I laid an egg in every case — the book not acknowledged, the letter unanswered. Though I had supported the ALP for years, I was no longer necessary — even an embarrassment — a nutty old amateur from the brotherhood of untouchables, otherwise poofs, carrying on about nuclear disarmament and that great money spinner uranium.

At the same time I wrote letters and sent the book to Thatcher, Reagan (the Australian Government's knight in shining armour) and Mitterrand (I had the letter to the Frenchman translated into idiomatic contemporary French, knowing that the French ignore any language but their own). I planned to have all these letters to the northern hemisphere published open in leading newspapers. They never appeared. I haven't even heard from the intermediaries whether they were received or forwarded.

At this point it will probably cross somebody's mind: significant, surely, that Patrick White, a crypto-commie, didn't get in touch with the Soviet. I was preparing to write when I received an invitation through the Soviet Embassy, Canberra, to fly to Moscow and address the Union of Soviet Writers. I needed a little time to think it over, but rang back the following day accepting, if I were allowed at the same time to talk to Gromyko. (I had in my mind's eye a picture of the Haydens on their Russian visit standing like lost souls in an art gallery. I was vain enough to think: would I be as lost as that?) I heard no more from the Russians. Perhaps they had spent all their money on the travel and entertaining of an Australian establishment composer. Music is less disturbing — a-political. Whereas those who deal in words can come up with a few unwelcome themes.

The moral of all this: it is futile for an individual to attempt to direct the leaders of the world along what he believes is the right track. (I have read that American law even considers it illegal — *apropos* Jesse Jackson's exploits in Cuba.) It can only be done if the peoples of the world unite. At least we are consolidating more and more. It is the only way we can overcome despair and the sense of futility so many of us are suffering from.

The Australian Aborigines, from whose metaphysics we whites can learn so much, have a saying, 'He who loses his dreaming is lost'. As I understand, 'dreaming' can be interpreted as his links with the past, his spirit life, his connections with tree, rock, landscape, his totems, in more sophisticated terms, his spirituality, God (however much it may shock some of us to hear that word, an affront to our intellectuality). As *I* see it, loss of faith, our 'dreaming', is the prime disaster which has overtaken most of the world in the latter part of the twentieth century. To me, and I believe millions of others, it is no longer possible to have faith in politicians who are ready to risk destroying the world for the money and power they delude themselves into thinking they will get out of this monstrous act.

Take our own politicians, the Prime Minister and so many of his supporters shrieking their heads off at the recent ALP Conference. His wife (probably a nice ordinary woman if she hadn't been caught up in the political grinder) now smiling plastic smiles as she promotes the theme of educating children in the preservation of an environment her husband is preparing to dig up and sell for the billions of dollars we shall get out of it. What double standards, what cynicism! It distresses me to think I voted for such hypocrites — that for years I supported a party which is selling out on our country. After Curtin and Chifley, what is there to choose between Menzies, Fraser — that great brooding cat as pictured recently in the press — and now Hawkie, screaming from under his cockatoo hairdo the platitudes he has got by heart. I gave up voting for Menzies. I never voted for Fraser. How could I after being inspired by Gough? I still had my hopes pinned to the ALP at the last election. I was invited to the inaugural speeches at the Sydney Opera House to provide a bit of window dressing. At a reception afterwards I was led up to the new Prime Minister. I brought up the subject of uranium. He appeared uneasy in spite of his political triumph, his coiffeur, and his sartorial splendour. He replied, 'Oh yes. Cliff Dolan will deal with that — a very good man'.

I still hope the party I have been supporting will rise from its fall. Or will this be humanly possible when the leaders we have trusted are joining with other maniacs to produce the grand explosion? Deterrence! More and more arms of increasing power will deter nobody. It will only lead to increased suspicion, lack of faith — and destruction.

It is not the prerogative of cocksure lawyer-politicians with a smattering of education and depraved, back-room scientists to decide whether we shall live or die. Life belongs to the people who live it, in many cases semi-educated, but with a store of instinct — intuitions — among whom I dare to include myself. I rise above my moments of deepest despair by remembering these millions of human beings.

When the Prime Minister and now his echo Mr Hayden assure us that the majority of Australians, realizing the benefits the sale of uranium will bring, support uranium policy, they are spattering us with bullshit, insulting our intelligence. They try to ignore the thousands who march in our peace rallies, the millions who are marching throughout the world: the women, the doctors, now even lawyers against uranium.

At the last Palm Sunday rally in Sydney I was shocked to hear Bill Hayden booed by the crowd. A couple of weeks before he turned, I wrote him a letter saying he was one of the few politicians I believed we could still trust. What a sucker he must have thought me!

The Prime Minister tells us politicians overseas look at him in amazement if he questions their uranium policy and their belief that you can safeguard its use. *Safeguard!* You can't safeguard anything in Australia, let alone the world. Anyhow, Hawkie pipes down when censured by his foreign peers. In spite of the hair-do and the well-tailored suit, the Australian inferiority complex surfaces. The bully-boy is got on side.

The alternatives to futility and despair are here around us. They don't only depend on the wrongly-called ordinary people I have referred to. There are important public figures, more than I can name, who have spoken out recently, at conferences, and through the media, and who will, I'm sure, continue speaking out, because they are men and women of integrity — Jeanette McHugh, for one — the two Jacks, Hallam and Mundey; Hallam, a refreshingly quiet man who has risked his political career by espousing the anti-uranium cause, and who is engaged in redressing the abuses to which pastoral Australia has been subjected; and Mundey, who has risen above diabolical treatment from his fellow workers and a shattering personal tragedy, to continue battling for justice for the underprivileged in my native city, and to ensure that petty crooks don't rule the roost. I must also mention Judith Wright the poet, and Faith Bandler, one of the most persuasive spokeswomen for the black people of Australia, who understands from personal experience that black and white *can* be brought together in peace and amity.

All races — all faiths — can, I feel, be brought together if we try. Like Faith Bandler, I know it from personal experience both here and in the world. We are certainly up against it in stiff-necked Australia. When I returned to live in my native land after World War II, we were raging against the Jewish 'reffos' of Central Europe. Later it became the Balts. There are still side swipes at the 'dagoes', invaluable throughout the country, and now of course there is perhaps the greatest rage of all against the new wave of Asians. In time all these resentments have more or less subsided and the more thoughtful among us have accepted the contributions to our life and culture these different races have made.

I would like to tell you of an incident which made a deep impression on me when I returned here to settle in 1946. I had come down to Sydney from Muswellbrook with a cousin. We shared a taxi from Central into the city. I dropped my cousin, who paid his share of the fare, while I took the taxi on to the hotel where I was booked in. There the driver expected me to pay the full fare. When I pointed out that the other passenger had paid half, the man stood on the kerb screaming, 'Go back to Germany! Go back to Germany!' Then I knew what it was like to be a reffo in Australia. I think it was this more than anything which persuaded me to write the novel *Riders in the Chariot*.

As a homosexual I have always known what it is to be an

outsider. It has given me added insight into the plight of the immigrant — the hate and contempt with which he is often received. We all have our contributions to make — whether in a bag shop, a deli, or as artists. I have lived for 43 years with a 'dago', a man of the greatest distinctions, whose wisdom has permeated my writing. We have made a joint contribution. So when we have come to our senses, we shall see that the Asians who have caused such a storm today, will have made theirs.

I don't know how many of you heard Bishop Tutu of South Africa speak when he came here recently. An inspired man. He made me understand the improbable condition of sainthood as I listened to him on my kitchen radio while doing the washing up. Persecuted by the unrepresentative government of his own country, he has risen above this persecution. He brushed aside a slap in the face he received from a Sydney Evangelical bigot. I don't claim to be a Christian — I have met too many bad ones — but might become a convert if Tutu remained around.

There is little to choose between religious and political bigotry. Bigotry is bigotry, an attitude, a frame of mind. There are those of us who are rigid in their adherence to a Labor Party which has sold out on its ideals as it has under the leadership of Hawke. To me it is unethical when a man turns his back on the most important moral issue in history. Those who cling to him are afraid the party may fall apart. I would not want to see the party disintegrate or the country endure another term of Liberal rule, because, whatever the faults of the ALP, it is better for those at the bottom of the social scale. However, I can't continue to accept the Hawke dictatorship when its support of a pro-uranium policy shows that its foundations are rotten.

So I propose to go along with a Nuclear Disarmament Party, the formation of which is underway, and which aims to provide candidates for the next Federal elections to the Senate and House of Representatives. The Nuclear Disarmament Party is a single issue party and its platform is as follows:

1. To close all foreign military bases in Australia.

2. To prohibit the stationing of nuclear weapons in Australia, or passage of nuclear weapons through Australian waters or airspace.

3. To terminate immediately all mining and export of Australian uranium, and to repudiate all commitments by previous Australian governments to mining, processing and export of uranium.

Facing the uranium issue honestly is what may save Australia and set an example to the world. It may give us back our 'Dreaming', our faith: as the Aborigines see it, in soil and country and spirit life; and for the whites of the Western world, our faith in one another. From murdering the Aborigine after our takeover of this continent, then initiating him into alcohol, and passing on venereal diseases and tuberculosis, we have now dispensed the deadlier disease which comes from the lust for uranium money. From now on it is our duty to start exorcising hate and suspicion; to unite — all of us — in creating faith in life and humankind.

RETURNING from his enthusiastically received speech at La Trobe University the week before, White addressed a packed Sydney Town Hall. The crowd welcomed him to the microphone with cheering and clapping. They hung on his every piercing word.

Hiroshima Day

1984

FELLOW CITIZENS — this is about WAR — the ferocious death's head that has been grinning at us down the decades — never more blatantly than in 1984 — when, if the arms race reaches a climax, the grin may well be wiped off the death's head itself — along with the faces of innocent, frivolous, unthinking humanity and this radiant earth on which it has been our privilege to live.

This, of course, is a frivolous statement on my part when so many people in this hall — in Australia — and throughout the world have been giving so much thought and time to averting the disaster of a nuclear war. Not yet enough of us, however — even though the evidence *against* war, both before and after Hiroshima, would *seem* to be enough.

Take World War II in Europe: Stalin admitted 20 million Russians were killed. It is believed the figure was higher, but the Russian dictator did not want to admit it because it would have reflected on his leadership.

Back in the 1950s Einstein, and Bertrand Russell the British philosopher, mathematician, and peace activist, foresaw the danger of nuclear war escalating into a universal holocaust. They issued a declaration which warned, 'Remember your humanity and forget all other things. Man's continued existence is in doubt.' Could you think of two nobler apostles of peace than Einstein and Russell? At the time when the declaration was made it was signed by Communists and non-Communists alike. The famous Russian physicist Markov still speaks with passion of the declaration. *I* urge all Australians, even the holy joggers and extrovert footballers, if a few syllables of this declaration should reach their ears, 'Remember your humanity. Forget all other things. Man's continued existence is in doubt...' These are the voices of Einstein and Bertrand Russell from out of the universe — not just that silly old bastard Patrick ranting his head off about something at a meeting.

To return to War, before it developed into the superconsumer — Helmuth von Moltke the elder, an architect of the modern German army, wrote in 1890, 'Woe to him who first sets fire to Europe.' In the trench warfare between 1914-18 millions were killed. The Battle of the Somme which began in 1916 and lasted from July to November, saw about 1,300,000 soldiers killed or wounded on both sides. There are Australians still alive who experienced this nightmare.

How right von Moltke was. What did World War I settle? Nothing. It was only a stage in the development of war. After Europe was set on fire it continued to smoulder. How did it start? Lloyd George, British Prime Minister towards the end of World War I, admitted, 'We all muddled into war...' It would be less alarming if we could say today we are still muddling, but the leaders of the superpowers seem heading towards it with the fixed grin of the death's head itself. The clash could occur at any moment.

The horrors of World War I did not prevent us getting into it again in 1939. This time certainly Hitler was responsible. There followed the devastation of London, Coventry, Hamburg, Dresden, Berlin. In the Pacific sphere, the climax came with Hiroshima and Nagasaki. Our gathering together tonight commemorates their destruction.

Alas, the habit of war will not let go. Our leaders are hooked on it. At the time it seemed to the more thoughtful that what happened at Hiroshima and Nagasaki was the peak of human bestiality. But here we are, set for it again. The results could be infinitely more horrendous, thanks to the perverted ingenuity of certain scientific 'geniuses'.

Michael Howard, one of the more objective historians of

war, recently wrote:

'I am an Englishman whose youth was passed in watching the dreadful onslaught of totalitarianism in Europe, and whose young manhood was passed in fighting it. I am a professional historian who has spent the last thirty years studying the phenomena of military power. I have noted the appetite of powerful states for more power to protect themselves, and the edge ideology can give to the appetite. I do not think I have any illusions about the Soviet Union. But when I hear some of my American friends speak of that country, when I note how their eyes glaze over, their voices drop an octave, and they grind out the word *the Soviets* in tones of gravelly hatred, I become really frightened...'

That perceptive American journalist and political analyst Thomas Powers has remarked, 'Statesmen thrive as long as war only threatens.' Looking back, I find that extraordinarily true. Like politicians when in opposition, they thump the drum, then so often shrink to pygmy size when in power and faced with reality.

What is reality? we may ask. Something different for everyone. Look at Reagan, the straw cowboy, and his buddy, Bush, flexing their muscles on the election trail, in their Texas hats, flanked by a couple of busty starlets. Such a set-up must mean reality for many American electors or it couldn't be practised so successfully. War, I feel, must be a celluloid adventure, a series of clips from *Gone with the Wind* or *Apocalypse Now,* for those who have not experienced it on their own soil, or anyway since away back in history.

For that matter, Australians haven't known war at home. True, there are the lists of friends and relatives who didn't come back from overseas and who, in many cases, remained a long-lasting source of grief, but our experience of war in Australia has only been peripheral, the bombing of Darwin in World War II, a pearling fleet sunk off Broome, and those Jap subs which entered Sydney Harbour, when, in the alarm which ensued, one of my great-aunts fell off her bed and broke a leg. Fringe events, with a dash of bathos.

Like so many Australians, Americans probably can't believe in war because *they* haven't been its target. War hasn't rolled through their back yards, crushing, disembowelling. They haven't seen their homes crumble, or neighbours and loved ones turned to corpses suppurating in familiar streets. *Un*like the Russians — millions killed, frozen, starved.

The British found out about it on their home ground in World War II — surviving only if they were lucky under the rubble created by bombs. Friends you had shared a joke with that evening, often could not be found next morning — after one of those rumbling nights of fug and farts, in the underground or your own cellar.

I experienced something of the Blitz on London. I know something of the starvation and humiliations of a country like Greece under occupation by a foreign power.

The pain, the horrors, the devastation, the hunger, the corruption, the rape, the adulteries of War... Alas, we are all to some extent to blame! That is one of the terrible truths. Germany can hardly deny that most Germans knew the Jews were being rounded up and carted off somewhere it was best not to think about. If any of us are to survive a nuclear holocaust, those survivors will know it happened because a majority of the world's population was too inert, too hedonistic, too ignorant, too complacently wealthy to organise timely resistance to the leaders who devised it.

I should have thought Hiroshima, back in the horse-and-buggy days of nuclear weapons, would be warning enough. For me the icon of Hiroshima I shall always remember is the figure of a man they saw standing naked amongst the ash and the tatters of human flesh in the black wastes of what had been his native city staring dazed at one of his eyeballs on the open palm of his extended hand. This could be the fate of any of us if we don't unite — you, or your father, uncle, son, standing in the wastes of what had been Sydney — at Lidcombe, say — or Maroubra — the Cross — Double Bay — Mosman — or wherever.

The extraordinary part is that President Reagan, his back-room scientists, and our own piddling politicians, of broken promises and immoral uranium policies, have never caught sight of this Hiroshima man. Or is it that they are so shocked by the sight and thought of the sacrificial figure that they are metaphorically blinded by his reality? It is easier to turn to the theories of deterrence and safeguards, and generally lick the arse of an imperious, materialistic ally who will continue manipulating his puppets for whatever purpose *he* sees fit.

None of this will *deter*. If we achieve anything it will be through the peoples of the world, and more and more of us are marshalling our forces in the cause of nuclear disarmament and peace.

All power in particular to the New Zealander* in withstanding the pressures put on him by the United States and faithless members of our own Government. May he and his peace supporters continue to resist. (Since I wrote this, I must say, one of our ministers seems to have seen the light.)

I don't know how many of you are aware of the Nuclear Disarmament Party which is being formed in Australia, and which aims to provide candidates for the next Federal Elections to the Senate and House of Representatives. It is a single issue party and its platform is as follows:

1. To close all foreign military bases in Australia.
2. To prohibit the stationing of nuclear weapons through Australian waters or airspace.
3. To terminate immediately all mining and export of Australian uranium, and to repudiate all commitments by previous Australian governments to mining, processing and export of uranium.

In this way Australia could set an example which those of like mind in other countries might follow, to share in the joys of LIFE instead of its extinction by nuclear war.

As A SUPPORTER of the New Zealand Labour Government's stand on nuclear ships, Patrick White was invited to Auckland to give out media Peace Prizes to journalists who had made contributions to the cause of peace. The event took place at Auckland's War Memorial Museum on 2 November.

Peace and Other Matters

1984

DEAR NEIGHBOURS, Perhaps a somewhat odd way to start an official speech — but I have never seen myself as an official — and I see *us* — New Zealanders and Australians — playing odd roles in human relationship in the late 20th Century. We are still in a sense folksy characters talking to one another across the back yard paling fence — or slamming the receiver down in temporary indignation. Our local recriminations are in the old style while we face together the global problems which threaten the world with disaster today. It comforts me — and many others of like mind in my country — that you are here across the Tasman — and that we can rely on you to support us in our ideals for the South Pacific and our resistance to the arrogant bullies of this world.

It is a great honour to be asked to come here to talk to you and present peace awards in a country which is working for peace as a necessity, not merely theorizing about it. We, more than you, are plagued by an establishment which wears two faces, which adopts a *pragmatic* attitude, to use a fashionable and ultimately meaningless word. Of course it really means that we must lick the arses of our American overlords. Increasing numbers of my fellow peace activists in Australia find this humiliating — unworthy of the Labor Government we elected. Consequently New Zealand's stand, not only that of your recently elected Labour Government, but the attitude of many New Zealand conservatives, has been an inspiration to us. If we could submerge our fears and suspicions, unity is what will save us. Perhaps this has already begun to happen, both at home and abroad, not necessarily at an ideological level, but a moral one — through the professions, artists, workers, and above all, the women of the world.

There are so many threads to disentangle when trying to analyse the reasons for a war that it is difficult to know where to begin. When it is over the planners can't explain adequately how it came about, except that in the words of Lloyd George after World War I, 'we all muddled into it'. Muddle is certainly the key to World War I and the muddy, bloody, personal slaughter of trench warfare. World War II, with its horrific climax at Hiroshima and Nagasaki, is more difficult to explain away. Admittedly we were all exhausted, but that was no reason for resorting to a solution so evil that, looking back it is hard to recover one's faith in humankind.

Surely we must all make every possible effort to resist being drawn into even greater madness in 1984 or *any* future date as the result of the arms race? Remember the Japanese mother looking for her baby in that first shambles, an infant the blast had torn from her breast, and at last finding what she describes as 'a little creature like a boiled octopus'. Remember the man I can never forget reading about, one of the most poignant symbols of destruction, despair and human degradation, the man standing naked on the wasteland of his home city — a Japanese Auckland or Wellington, let us imagine — staring dazed at one of his own eyes lying on the palm of his open hand.

But remember the bombs which destroyed Hiroshima and Nagasaki were only a trial run for the desolation World War III will inflict on our planet if we, the people of the world, allow megalomaniac leaders to force it on us — the Reagans, the Thatchers, the Mitterrands heading the list — with many lesser stars seduced by the idea of power and perks accruing from a superwar.

Those vainglorious leaders who see their nation's and their own strength measured in terms of success at sport, athletics and yacht racing are bound to fall on their faces in the end. Pour money into sport and you'll get the votes, but the vote of the mindless. The shrunken belly is the vote you must court.

The impoverished, the unemployed, the despairing, emergent young in an affluent society are the key to what is most important — PEACE. Bread is more substantial than games, and faith in the moral value of their leaders most substantial of all. Let us resist the easy way of feeding illusions to the young — adults too, for that matter. One of the grand illusions of the politician is the hope that uranium can be made safe. There is this constant talk about 'safeguards', but what price safeguards when a cargo of plutonium is sunk off the Belgian coast. Of course they then come out with the glib assertion that it will do no harm. There is accident after accident in the United States. Lucas Heights in Sydney — no harm — but they hush it up till after a Government conference. Windscale in Britain — they change the place-name, but they can't do away with the high incidence of leukaemia in children in that part of the country. Safeguards! Whom can we trust? What about the cargo of plutonium bound for Japan which sailed from the French port of Cherbourg heading for the Panama Canal under American escort? Isn't this a superb example of international hypocrisy? Dollars before anything. Is it any wonder that our young are disillusioned — that they have lost interest in politics (anyway, most youthful Australians have) when, if we can revive their interest and trust, they could help in so many positive ways to arrest the rot with which this glorious world is riddled.

Out of a conference on uranium organised in Canberra last year by Dr Michael Denborough of the ANU, attended by scientists from the United States, Russia, Britain, Australia, a Greenie from Germany, an American soldier who played an important part in the Vietnam War, and various peace activists, a Nuclear Disarmament Party has evolved in Australia.

Briefly, it is a single-issue political party which aims to do something about the nuclear threat by providing candidates for the Senate at the next federal elections.

The party's platform is:

1. To close all foreign military bases in Australia.
2. To prohibit the stationing in Australia or the passage

through Australian waters or airspace of any nuclear weapons.

3. To terminate immediately all mining and export of uranium, and to repudiate all commitments by previous governments to the mining, processing and exporting of uranium.

There have been the usual squabbles amongst the members of this new party, but I believe we have finally firmed and formed. During our trials, we have received great stimulus from you in New Zealand. I hope we can support each other in the South Pacific. I feel that this support will be more sincere than that of others who will now be horning in on us: Admiral Crowe of the US, the Baroness Young propelled from British Foreign Affairs to a conference at Noumea with elocution enough to out-Thatcher Thatcher, and Big Mummy herself dragging her recalcitrant colonial children back under the British umbrella. I find this pathetic in 1984 in the day of David Lange and his independent stand. I like to think that this gallant man has no need of Lady Young, Admiral Crowe, the Privy Council or any other baits. If we want to hang on to our independence, we of the South Pacific must wash these persons out of our hair. I believe that the more radical anti-nuclear Australians, Mr Lange's New Zealanders, and the less powerful members of the South Pacific alliance can get together and develop positive policies. Take, for instance, the Solomon Islanders and their resistance to the American tuna pirates. The islanders were great. All the more distressing that Mr Somare could only offer that weary *cliché*, 'We support you in principle...' Come on, Mr Somare, remember you were a human being before you became a politician.

Here I'm going to digress for a moment. Some of you will see it as self-indulgence, nostalgia, sentimentality. However it illuminates the personal link I have with our South Pacific. When I was a child of five to six there was a Solomon Islander working for my family in Sydney, Solomon Rakooka (Sol), a rorty character who had been a seaman earlier in life. He had a boxful of treasures from Buenos Aires and Rio which he would bring out to show to my admiring self. He used to bring me home from kindergarten, my small white hand in his large black spongy one as he helped me aboard the tram. He was always around in the Douanier Rousseau garden of my childhood. We planted a mango stone together. We watered it. We dug it up every other day to see whether it had germinated. It had. What happened to our mango I can't remember. It probably died of too much loving care from our black and white alliance. And the alliance broke up, destroyed by grog and prostitutes. Sol had to go. We loved him. We all cried when he walked down the drive for the last time in his badly fitting army boots.

I introduce this episode because it leaves me with a personal duty — my duty to the South Pacific — like a white colonist's duty to the Australian Aborigines — my duty to the so-called ethnics in these days of rage from certain quarters against the Asians — the rage in past decades against dagoes, Jewish reffos, Balts — and the rest of those we see when we come to our senses have contributed immeasurably to our culture.

Today in my own country there is a particularly dangerous situation created by a body sometimes referred to as the New Right — in other words the New Fascists. Still only morally distasteful the movement could very easily explode in physical violence and distract our attention from the great issues of nuclear disarmament, global peace, and starving nations.

At this moment there is a tensely unreal atmosphere in the Western world — the miasma created by pending political elections — in Hawke's Australia — in Reagan's Disneyland — and the tottering of Thatcher's sick empire. The dichotomy between the classes, between rich and poor, which one likes to think diminished in the Western democracies, is still with us. The Australian poet Robert Gray reminds us very vividly:

I have been in Petticoat Lane — pushing by through narrow, stacked alleys,
amongst the tons of rotting garbage for sale, and have seen
    the really poor.
Those people seemed just dangling paper dolls threaded onto
    a genetic string —
the genes of poverty, starch, lack of sun,
and stunted, hopeless spirit everywhere. Their crossed eyes
    warts, twisted faces, snaggle teeth,
drunkenness were Dickens still, in '70 something
    again in '82. People in greasy rags, on crutches, weeding
wet butts from the gutter, wild-eyed,
spiky-haired, foul-muttering.
The women were shaped like slapped-together piles of clay.
    They scrabble amongst junk, scratching themselves
                    viciously
shouting and oblivious...
What is such an evil, but the continuing effect
    of Capital's Stalinism?
Enclosure, as John Clare has said, lets not a thing remain.
And then, an hour later, in the West End I found
how much worse I thought the fleshy,
askance meringue-coloured, prissy-lipped upperclass face —
    so sleek
in *its* obliviousness.
People go rotten with culture, also.

After the polls which are hanging over the Democracies at the end of 1984, shall we recover our balance, I wonder, our capacity for honest behaviour? There are already signs of wavering — Mr Lange's hint that New Zealand may allow the presence of American warships if they can be proved safe. American warships on a recent visit to Melbourne were cursed and warned off by *one* retired wharfie who claimed to represent a million anti-nuclear Australians. In Adelaide a mayoral reception was given for the officers and men of the visiting warships. New York and Boston are more realistic in not allowing nuclear warships access to their harbours.

That most civilised country France is notoriously un-civilised where her own interests are concerned. If her tests in the Pacific are safe, why can they not be carried out in her homeland, as suggested by Colombia? Everywhere a brood-ing deceit — the United States and China waiting to do deals after the American election. One nation waiting to blackmail another as soon as an opportunity arises. Fear that the Amer-ican bully may boycott New Zealand products if the smaller country does not obey. Is there any reason why Russia, China, or the South East Asian countries would not buy New Zealand products? All is fair in commerce and pseudo-love.

If we met one another with open hands and sincere inten-tions, instead of clenched fists and the tatty little, outdated ANZUS treaty, it is possible we might achieve the peace the majority of us desire.

Again I'm going to quote a poem by the Australian poet Robert Gray, *To the master Dōgen Zenji* (who lived from AD 1200-1253).

> He said, All that's important
> is the ordinary things.
> Making the fire
> to boil some bathwater, pounding rice, pulling the weeds
> and knocking dirt out of their roots,
> or pouring tea — those blown scarves,
> a moment, more beautiful than the drapery
> in paintings by a Master.
> — 'It is this world of the *dharmas*,
> (the atoms)
> which is the Diamond.'

For those who may be mystified, *dharma* is the Buddhist truth, the Hindu moral law; again the atoms are those small, ordinary things, as well as the truth, the Diamond being the acme of pure Truth.

The ordinary things — simplicity and plain speech such as politicians forget is spoken by plain people in ordinary life could save this world of ours.

Let's give it a go!

SINCE 1985 Sydneysiders have argued for and against the aesthetics, the economics and the electoral sense of having a monorail link, owned by the multi-national TNT, running above Sydney streets and down to the entertainment complex at Darling Harbour. Protest rallies were frequent and always colourful, drawing at times crowds of 10,000 people. White was one of the dedicated supporters of the vigorous, but for the moment at least, defeated, anti-monorail campaign.

The opera version of Patrick White's novel *Voss* opened at the 1986 Adelaide Festival of Arts in March, and at the Sydney Opera House in June.

Monsterail

1986

It seems to me that the Monsterail, ugly, expensive, and dangerous though it will be, as well as congesting already narrow streets, is only the fringe of what could turn out to be one of the major physical and moral disasters of this Mate-land in which we live. Devised by Führer Wran and Gauleiter Brereton* in conjunction with Askin's knight and Wran's accomplice Sir Peter Abeles*, we are frequently told the monstrous rail will make life easier for the people. It was thought up by the Mates for their vainglory and profit in connection with the Chinese connection of Hooker/Harrah*, to serve the Darling Harbour Casino. I can't see how anybody who has visited Las Vegas, as our politicians do, would want to foist such a monster on us. I am not talking about that part of the desert city which caters exclusively for the rich with entertainments and vulgar splendour. But the desperate side of this hell on earth, the gaming rooms with their suffocating, stale air, lit the twenty-four hours with a dim red light outside, the cluster of crummy rooming houses and pawnshops, where the unsuccessful hang out, hoping they can scrape enough together for one last try. It is the scene of broken lives, and often suicide. All this is being prepared for us by the mates who run this Mate-land of ours. Do we, my fellow citizens, want to condone such an enterprise? Or do we feel that we too, have some responsibility for what happens to our city? Let us show we have by first banning the Monster-rail and then resisting, as far as we can, the development of the Darling Harbour Casino, forced on us by dictatorial leaders with no regard for democratic procedure.

THIS WAS the United Nations International Year of Peace, and a symposium was organized in Canberra on 11 November to discuss 'the precision of our words and the force of our imagination' in a nuclear age. Patrick White, together with sixty other writers, spoke to a full hall in the Australian Defence Force Academy. As a result of this symposium initiated by academics David Headon and Dorothy Green, Writers Against Nuclear Arms (WANA) was formed.

White's most recent novel, *Memoirs of Many in One*, was published in this year.

Imagining the Real

1986

W<small>HEN</small> I was asked to come to Canberra and talk about 'Writing in the Nuclear Age' I got an attack of the cold shudders. Not because one knows nuclear war could mean the world's total destruction. Rather it was the prospect of talking. I am an awkward talker. An old-fashioned writer. I have not been trained to jet round the world reading and talking. I have always refused invitations of that kind. On this occasion I would have chosen to shirk my responsibility. But realised I couldn't. Too much shirking has been going on in this country — amongst politicians, the wealthy, athletes, sportsmen. Even writers, to be candid. But we'll come back to that later. We are invited here to imagine the real. I must say I enjoy the irony of taking part in such a function in the most unreal city in Australia, over-ripe with the hypocrisy of politics and diplomacy.

How can we begin to join with other nations in calling the bluff of that arch-hypocrite President Reagan, our official ally, and the French destructors of the South Pacific if we still have so much to tidy up at home? I shall no doubt be pounced on for leaving out the Soviet Anti-Christ from among those I criticise, but for all their Russian faults I can't ignore signs of sincerity in the Soviet leader absent from his American counterpart and the xenophobe French.

For that matter I have to look fairly hard for signs of sincerity in our own politicians — in their uranium policy, their attitude to Aborigines, American bases, and the lengths to which they go to distract our attention from the real by laying on yacht races, staging State funerals as theatrical functions or political events, or a banquet in honour of a venerable character whose innate honesty would, they hoped, disguise the corruption and guile of those surrounding him. In particular our homespun leaders are relying on the massive injection of unreality they are preparing for us in 1988 — tall ships, casinos, and stadiums to keep us quiet with thrilling displays of brutality. I like to think that many of those Australians usually referred to rather insultingly as 'ordinary' will size up the superfluities and omissions, and that some of our writers will alert their more innocent fellows to the danger of circuses in the age of nuclear threats.

How can any of us who have lived through the period of Hiroshima and Nagasaki accept the preparations for another holocaust by Reagan and his satellites? I find it difficult to understand how even younger citizens of the world, when faced with the history and images of the two martyred Japanese cities, do not react with a more personal horror — to those tatters of humanity — the grey rags of skin — flesh where the flies bred maggots in unprotected wounds — deformed limbs — inflated scars.

I only talk about the living. Many had vanished into the air and were never seen again — after the *baby* bombs. And now vast stockpiles are being stored up for the next round. Only a short time ago Chernobyl demonstrated the effects of radiation in Europe. Both American and Russian scientists have asserted that in the event of a nuclear winter medical resources will not be able to cope with the survivors.

Yet, so many Australians suffer from complacency. They kid themselves they are safe, while politicians continue squabbling about allowances, residences, numbers, who is Left, Right, or Centre, grow fat on steak and Chardonnay, and prepare blow-waves and suiting for the next TV appearances. Writers have an increasing responsibility towards this country. A lot of you have the qualities I don't possess — you are intellectuals, academics. At my worst, I am a doodler; at my best, I like to think a kind of bricklayer or stonemason. Put together, our joint qualities can assault those I increasingly suspect — the politicians and megalomaniacs.

However, time can be lost now that distance has telescoped; credulousness, alas, is with us still. I pray that enough of you have escaped infection from the writers' disease of talking about ourselves — all that yakker about 'how I work'. It's more important to get on and *do* in this dangerous age.

And beware the glittering prizes! These can blunt the cutting edge — politicians' ploys to fuel a fertile ego and truss you in their web. They can wreck your life. As I know from experience. A capricious pin poised above your head. One prick and you're a goner. You've lost friends and gained flatterers.

The other day I read an anecdote told by a former lover of the American film and stage actress Gloria Grahame, who towards the end of her life was awarded an Oscar for her performance in the film *The Bad and the Beautiful*. Soon after she died of a malignant tumour. But at least she had time to make the memorable remark, 'I can't stand the sight of Ronnie Reagan, I'd like to stick my Oscar up his ass'.

I admire Gloria's frankness, and share her disgust for the man who leads his supporting choirs in *Onward Christian Soldiers* while preparing for Armageddon.

Reagan seems to me a perfect example of somebody unable to imagine the real. What he does imagine is that he is acting for the good of the world, by which he means the American people. So he continues carrying out nuclear tests in the Nevada deserts. He closes his eyes whenever possible to nuclear leaks in various parts of his territory. Britain would like to ignore her *polluting* of the Irish Sea with nuclear waste. The Soviets at least were unable to conceal Chernobyl or their maimed submarine off Bermuda.

In Australia the technological crime of Maralinga* provided a slight foretaste of the future, and a warning not to trust our allies. Puppets of the English earlier in history, we found ourselves cast in the same role for the Maralinga experiment, thanks to our prime minister's infatuation for his monarch. Could the same thing happen today? Strange things do, and the Queen of England — I refuse to call her the Queen of Aus-

tralia — enjoys lingering here with her ambassador extraordinary, Bully Boy Philip, and members of her spawning
family beloved of subscribers to the *Women's Weekly.* Given
a bolt-hole, even anachronistic royalty might fit into the
nuclear jigsaw, for it is clear no one can escape a nuclear
future. Look at the way our defences went down recently at
Fremantle and Garden Island before those ambiguous warships. Who cares what you let in if the wallet and the cod-
piece are full?

Catching a politician's ear is a trick I've never mastered.
They see me, I suspect, as a ratbag to use and discard. A few
years ago when some of ours were leaving for Greece I begged
them to notice what has happened to the Saronic Gulf as they
were driven in their VIP limos to lunches and dinners in and
around Athens. By now the situation has worsened as it has
in the bays and along the coasts of Australia. The sludge of
progress laps at the shores of Homer's Aegean. The fish are
poisoned or fished out. The Greeks hate the tourists coaxed
in to prop up their economy. And the same will happen in
Australia. In the scramble after mineral wealth in the nuclear
age, our country's beauty will be scarred, her spirit estranged
by developers and their touts, the political non-planners.
Provided we miss some of the more disastrous effects of a
consuming war, the Australians, like the Greeks, will have come
to hate the sight of tourists, Americans to fill our resorts and
casinos, Japanese to cuddle koalas and wombats, and inhabit
colonies designed for their own geriatrics.

It may seem as though I've strayed from our theme, but
do we ever leave it, really — now that we know it's not so
distant — there in the ever-disturbed Nevada deserts with their
hell-hole Las Vegas, so impressive to Australian politicians;
the obscene, bacon-coloured Florida; the North Atlantic and
Pacific Oceans — over all of which Ronnie reigns.

Having introduced the B-Grade-movie President as a fun-
damentalist urging his Christian cohorts into Star Wars, it may
shock some of you if *I* turn to religion at the end. But I must;
the spirit of the land demands it. Actually I believe in prayer
more than Church dogma. I believe in our country more than

in sad little man-made boxes, or the equally insubstantial, Anglo-American mansions of our copy-cat plutocracy. I've got to admit my prayers sometimes go unanswered, but that doesn't mean I don't keep on at it:

I pray that we may act honourably at home and abroad; that our Aborigines receive the justice owing to them; that black and white live together in harmony; that we may concentrate, without further shilly-shally, on the vital projects of soil and water conservation; and that we may open the eyes of increasing numbers of our fellow countrymen to the universal issues of nuclear disarmament and peace.

T HIS TEXT was originally read by White direct to
Channel 9 cameras and filmed for Australia Day
by George Negus of *Good Morning Australia*. But
only short 'grabs' were ever used. So White offered it
to the small Canberra magazine *Blast*, which printed
it in full.

Three Uneasy Pieces had been rushed out at the end
of 1987 by Pascoe Publishing so that White could keep
to his intention of having no new work published
or presented during the Bicentenary.

The Bicentenary

1988

W<small>HY DID</small> I refuse to have any of my own work performed or published during the Bi?

The whole idea of the Bicentenary had been troubling me for some time. There was too little I could feel proud of in our past. Even less in our present — too many dishonest politicians, and too many vulgar philistine organisers piling the bullshit higher and higher. So I decided to have nothing to do with it. In 1987 I had success with a play in Adelaide. Sydney wanted it for the 1988 Festival, so did one of the theatres in Perth, so did the Royal Theatre Company in Brisbane. I refused all these.

A literary magazine to which I was persuaded to contribute some pieces in 1987 was due out last November. A Penguin Australia Anthology. When this was kept back till March 1988 — obviously a Bi-Centennial project — I withdrew my pieces and they were brought out by a small, independent Victorian publisher before Christmas. A triumph of quick and efficient publishing. And one in the eye for those who had lied to me. I can't stand liars.

Aborigines

More than anything, it was the need for justice for the Aborigines which put me against the Bi. Very little has been done to give them a sense of security in the country we invaded. In spite of a lot of last-minute, face-saving claptrap from the Prime Minister — one of the greatest bull artists ever. Aborigines may not be shot and poisoned as they were in the early days of colonisation, but there are subtler ways of disposing of them. They can be induced to take their own lives by the psychic torments they undergo in police cells. It's usually put down to drugs or drink — and some of them are on with these — they learnt it from the whites. In a town like Walgett prestigious white characters can be seen reeling about the streets on important occasions. In my boyhood when I used to go there to my uncle's sheep station on the Barwon, and he drove me in his buggy past the shanties on the outskirts of town, he said, 'There's nothing you can do for these people'. I was fond of my uncle, so I dismissed the blacks from mind till years after, I started to think — and met numbers of impressive black leaders — as well as girls and young men graduating as teachers — and through involvement with the Aboriginal Islander Dance Company. The Aborigines produce dazzling performing artists and painters.

Justice

Not only for Aborigines — we need justice for the poor, the disillusioned young, for the aged (take those old people turned out of their lodgings in this brash city to make way for tourists), justice for the mentally ill who are forced into a dubious alternative lifestyle by the closure of mental hospitals.

Democracy

The Bicentennial circus tends to hide from us the fact that we are no longer a democracy. We are a country run for and by millionaires and by a Prime Minister who toadies to them. Certainly there are politicians we can still admire — Bill Hayden, who emerges with dignity out of some of the dirtier situations his superiors don't want to tackle — Tom Uren, another one in the true Labor mould — Barry Jones, too civilised to please his colleagues. Outside Parliament there are others the despairing can look up to: Frank Costigan of the famous Commission who saw too much to appeal to those involved, he was kicked out (mediocrity is safer). There's the magnificent Ted Wheelwright, whose economic advice is asked, but not taken, or only too late. Nugget Coombs, who has given most of his life working for the Aborigines. Jack Mundey is a great battler for justice. Helen Caldicott, the firebrand whose warnings on nuclear issues are ignored by a Government which is selling uranium to the self-centred, eternally xenophobic French.

Australia the Subservient

Perhaps most humiliating of all, the Bicentennial celebrations demonstrate that Australia is intended to remain subservient — whether to the Americans, the Japanese, or most insidiously, the English. The Royal Goons will be with us most of the year. Queen Betty England is invited to open the 'concept' of Darling Harbour, and she and her bully boy will be at the inflated/ruinous Parliament House. The Princess Royal will be in her element amongst the horses at Sydney Agricultural Show. Charlie is being whisked up to play polo at Packer's* Place. When I pointed out to one of Charlie's loyal Australian subjects they may try to force him on us as Governor General, she said, 'It might save his marriage'. The same good soul came out with, 'Mr Hawke's for the little people'. Oh yeah? He's for his millionaires — for Packer who gave the solid gold birthday at which all his Labor mates turned up in their sequinned glory — Hawkie's for Bondie*, that great Australian of the America's Cup who is giving us a ship to celebrate the Bi, a university to preach the Bond gospel in, and who hovers over the corpse of democratic Chile like an obscene Blowie*. Bondie and Hawkie complement each other. Hawkie the would-be super statesman quacking round the globe high above ordinary mortals. Bondie, tycoon extraordinary, whose symbol floats above us in the shape of that bloated tourist balloon. Which of the mates will be the first to fall?

Tourism

All those countries which have needed tourism to bolster up their economy have regretted and been wrecked by it — aesthetically and morally. Take Greece, Spain, Italy and Southern France. They have all ended up hating the tourists who pollute them with plastic rubbish and exhaust fumes, and destroy their peace. Then, there's the casinos our politicians hanker after. For me a casino represents the tower of ruin and destruction — whether it's Wrest Point, with housewives in cardies* gambling away the housekeeping money, the dusty boredom of Monte Carlo, or the real red hell of Las Vegas at any hour of the day.

I can't see any good coming out of the Bicentenary for our country as a whole — only for the greedy conmen. I'm not alone in believing this. There are many thoughtful down-to-earth Australians who share my opinion. Circuses don't solve serious problems. When the tents are taken down, we'll be left with the dark, the emptiness — and probably a two-dollar loaf.

ENTHUSIASTICALLY received by audiences at Melbourne's La Trobe University, White visited them for a second time. Many of his remarks again provoked the reaction of 'bitter old man' from the media and cheers and claps from the students.

A Sense of Integrity

1988

As an epigraph I'm going to quote from a poem by the Australian poet Robert Gray. Some of you will have heard me quote from the same poem a few years ago. It is as relevant today as it was then. It will be as relevant a thousand years hence if the world survives. *To the master Dōgen Zenji* (who lived from AD 1200-1253).

> He said, All that's important
> is the ordinary things.
> Making the fire
> to boil some bathwater, pounding rice, pulling the weeds
> and knocking dirt out of their roots,
> or pouring tea — those blown scarves,
> a moment, more beautiful than the drapery
> in paintings by a Master.
> — 'It is this world of the *dharmas*,
> (the atoms)
> which is the Diamond.'

For those who may be mystified, Dharma is the Buddhist truth, the Hindu moral law; again the atoms are those small ordinary things, as well as the truth, the diamond being the acme of pure truth.

And so to a sense of integrity — in particular our own.

I'm going to pinch a remark made by that international man of theatre Peter Brook who was in Australia earlier this year to present his version of the epic *Mahabarata*. He has said, 'The moment a society wishes to give an official version of itself, it becomes a lie'. This is exactly what has happened in the year of the Bicentenary — which is also the year of the great Australian lie. Not that it hasn't had its positive, stimulating moments — the arrival of the ships in Sydney Harbour for instance, when for a few hours Australians seemed to forget their squabbles and to become more or less reconciled to one another. This already seems a long time ago. Since then we have been all out for the jugular in one another's throats. Perhaps it's normal in a jungle where the human beast is the most savage of all — where, for all our rationalising and material progress, we more or less take it for granted that our behaviour shall be sustained by lies.

It starts in childhood, where the child may be taught it is wrong to lie, yet any intelligent child can see that the parents are in many cases lying to each other — that they also see fit to lie to their children when it suits them — sometimes in all good faith to protect them from the realities of life.

So the trivial childhood lies develop naturally enough into the poisonous political and national lies of adulthood.

Let's take a look at some of the more trivial lies before facing up to the real shockers. A large proportion of grown Australians remain children at heart — I see them as kidults. That's why they're so easily deceived by politicians, developers, organisers of festivals, and that is why they fail to dig the real purpose of a giant circus like the Bi. Over and over they're taken in by what I call the weather lie. For instance we're frequently not told there's bad weather in the offing if it might interfere with the rites of the sacred long weekend — might upset the holiday-makers and the proprietors of tourist accommodation. We're not told about the pending storms which could affect attendance at sporting fixtures — though today the sight of thugs writhing in the mud and bashing the hell out of one another in the name of sport has perhaps become part of our national 'coltcher' — as well as a lucrative business.

Still on weather: its natural turbulence is described as 'freak storms' and 'flash flooding'. If we persuade ourselves that regular occurrences are unusual, it absolves us from diverting floodwaters into channels where they won't damage property and can be put to some agricultural use. We tell our-selves, it may not happen again, anyway for some time. Apathy is more comfortable than responsibility.

Intellectuals may expect a welter of philosophical overtones in a talk like this, but I feel I must keep my nose to the ground in painting the portrait of a kidult society.

A great number of Australians always seem to be running to or from somewhere — city to surf in my native city — capital to capital — sometimes in the name of charity or to advertise a product. But running, or driving cars across the country, fast or vintage, or flogging camels across deserts. Riders forcing their mounts over a terrain rough enough to break a horse's leg or maim it for life. This passion for perpetual motion — is it perhaps for fear that we may have to sit down and face reality if we don't keep going?

The ad-men are more than anything to blame — persuad-ing once respected politicians, sober judges, picturesque pro-fessors, into the endorsing racket, into launching, into being seen. Why do they do it? They surely don't need to add to their already considerable perks? Being seen is the great enticement. At the trendy restaurants the nosh experts are promoting. They're all in it together. It would seem that these personalities are terrified of spending a night at home. Might look as though they are failures. Or dead. This frame of mind was rife in the U.S. in the 1930s. And now it has caught on in Oz as we become increasingly Americanised. Those who can't afford to go on the town every night and are forced to stay at home with a book may finally bring us closer to the civilisation we haven't yet got. Books — silence — are civilis-ing. So are domesticity and food — not the latest wave of restaurant food. All great civilisations have been based on food — middle class and peasant cooking which demand long and loving attention, not a doctrine to appeal to the self-important, chasing after publicity and honours. The scramble for honours is such that by now it's an honour not to have one.

A nation in the true sense isn't born of self-congratulation and the accumulation of often ill-gotten and unequally dis-tributed wealth. I suppose I'll be condemned as a miserable

Jeremiah if I say it is born of suffering. Australians have suffered in the past, which they tend to forget now that they're on with the bonfires — the champagne (the ad-man's magic lure) and the festivals. Even an occasion commemorating the horrors of Hiroshima has to be turned into a festival of sorts, with entertainers hired, often at great expense, to keep the kidult mourners amused.

In a society where there has been such a serious lapse in integrity, our politicians' attitude to uranium isn't surprising: increase mining, increase our sales of yellowcake (under supervisions, we are told) and now Senator Button's enrichment plan. Enrichment, indeed! But what price the ideals we once thought our government had? I would like to quote from a remarkable book *The Day of Judgment* by Salvatore Satta, a great Italian jurist of Sardinian origin, appointed to decontaminate Italian law after the Mussolini era. Satta says of a certain character in his book, 'In the law he had discovered the self-confidence that had eluded him in life, and was naturally led to mistake the law for life itself'. This could apply equally to politicians. It is not uncommon for a polly, in the course of serving those who elected him, to forget that life isn't politics.

Man is a frail creature, frailer than ever as we are sucked into an electronics age. We were warned of what was to come as early as 1974 by the British journalist Peter Laurie in an article in the *New Scientist* on brain-saving technology. By 1974 it was estimated that all significant American wealth was produced by just 20 per cent of its people. The rest of the work force was relegated to pretend jobs. To quote Laurie in the same article of 1974, 'A recent symposium on *The Computer in the Year Two Thousand* suggested that by the end of the century, there would be left a small percentage of the population, probably between 5 and 10 per cent, comprising the scientists, technologists, educators, managers, and planners, upon whom the smooth working of a society based on the extensive use of computers, would depend'. What happens to the rest is not difficult to foresee: a swift return to feudalism or an electronic variation of it, in which the elite and the masses are not even bound together by mutual usefulness, however one-sided it might be.

How does pure little Oz stand in the age of electronic feudalism? Rumours of a fortress-like surveillance headquarters and information bank in Canberra with branches in capital cities float around the country threatening our privacy at every aspect of our lives. Investigated by two responsible Ministers the situation appears to be the fantasy of an irresponsible fanatic. In any case, such intelligence aids are hardly necessary when we have Pine Gap, the facility we share with our dubious allies the Yanks, which can monitor not only the Soviet Union, but a number of other countries as well, and has the capacity to investigate Australians if it chooses.

So much for technology which some of our politicians and scientists exalt. Perhaps they will benefit by it. The enslaved populace certainly will not. The masters will continue to hoodwink the more innocent by telling them they have the best economy, the tallest tower, the cosiest casino, the greatest cricketer or swimmer. On top of the Bi, which is going to leave us all but broke, they have started babbling about the Games, when any city which has hosted the Olympic Games in recent years has regretted it both physically and financially.

While we are harping on what is best, I am going to promote as shamelessly as an A.B.C. radio ad — a cheese, believe it or not. It delights me to think we have in the Gippsland Blue a product I can honestly proclaim best in the world. Not a racehorse or a boxer, but a humble, civilising cheese.

After that little outburst let's go back a few years in time.

Moral distinction is probably a quality one is born with — nothing to do with formal education or class. Our Prime Minister Ben Chifley had it.

In a recent letter to a newspaper Sascha Taylor describes a goodwill visit paid by Chifley to the Queensland town of Longreach in 1947. The Prime Minister travelled alone by the normal rail service. Taylor's job was to cover the visit for the local newspaper. After the evening function, she strolled with Chifley back to his hotel. There was no sign of life in the foyer except for an elderly drunk. 'Chif' stopped to have a few words

with him, then, Sascha says, 'wished us both goodnight and
went upstairs to his room — a calm, self-contained, solitary
figure'.

Sascha goes on to say, 'It is hard to believe that this was
our Prime Minister a mere forty years ago. One wonders —
do today's private jets and army of minders, advisers and
bureaucrats make for better government, or only more government? How, in the space of only 40 years, did it all get so much
out of control?'

My answer to Sascha Taylor would be through the worship
of money as power and aping our American masters. On a
recent visit to Austin, Texas, hosted by a millionaire property
developer of the crudest tastes, Prime Minister Hawke con-
fessed he had never been made to feel at home so quickly.
Hawkie was no doubt reminded of his supporting cast of vul-
garian millionaires back in Oz. Would Chifley have succumbed
in 1988? I doubt it. He had his own innate honesty on side,
and a genuine concern for the people.

Here's a *cri de coeur* I hope may reach out far and wide.
DON'T DO IT, BILL*. You've been sacrificed once to Hawke.
Don't let it happen a second time. Years ago, before too much
falsification set in, I was privileged to speak from the same
platform as Bill Hayden — in Brizzy* of all places. Over the
years, events have temporarily come between us, but I respect
him for his persistence and sincerity. I wouldn't like to see
Yarralumla wreck my respect for an honourable man. So I
repeat, *DON'T DO IT, BILL HAYDEN, DON'T DO IT.*

I am accused of being an angry, bitter old man. Not surprising the earth is angry. Have you noticed every time there
is a nuclear test at Moruroa, there is an earthquake, or a
volcano erupts, somewhere in the Pacific zone?

So I am angry. If the earth is angry, the human beings who
inhabit it have cause to be angry too. Unless a superpower
or hidden talent of a lesser nation succeeds in destroying us,
we must all, in the years to come, work towards a civilisation based on humanity. Our creed, as I pray regularly (prayer
does rub off on someone somewhere) — I pray that we may
care for the sick as human beings, not mere charts on a hospi-

tal bed, or a body with a drip attached to it — I pray that we may feed, not only the starving nations, but the starving in our midst — that we may recognise the needs of our neglected old people and our disillusioned youth — comfort the failed — the humiliated — the deranged — remove fear from the threatened — the frightened — eliminate torture — and see that the poor and blacks receive the justice so often denied them — throughout the world — around Australia — and in our cities with their mix of sophisticated corruption and childish values. Follow the path of humility and humanity, and Australia might develop a civilisation worthy of the name. I believe most people hunger after spirituality, even if that hunger remains in many cases unconscious. If those who dragoon us ignore that longing of the human psyche, they are running a great risk. The sense of real purpose — the life force — could be expelled from a society whose leaders are obsessed by money, muscle, and machinery. That society could — quite simply — die.

Credo

1988

Unless you are one of the living dead, you'll have to write another will and another, always another...So, too, unless you've given up on life before time finally escapes, you will put together another Credo.

I am coming to believe, not in God, but a Divine Presence of which Jesus, the Jewish prophets, the Buddha, Mahatma Gandhi and Co. are the more comprehensible manifestations. This Presence controls us but only to a certain degree: life is what we, its components, make it. Hence the existence of megal-omaniac politicians, dictators, mafia millionaires, greedy landlords, rapists, murderers, self-obsessed spouses within the same scheme which embraces the Teresas, St. John of the Cross, Thomas Merton, and others who continue to speak to us out of the historic waxwork-museum — all these along with the anony-mous who lift us from the gutters, wiping the vomit from our lips, who comfort us as our limbs lie paralysed on the pavement, feed us within their limited means, and close our eyes — these humble everyday saints created for our consolation by the same mysterious universal Presence ignored, cursed, derided, or intermittently worshipped by the human race.

Notes

*indicated by * in text*

Civilisation, Money and Concrete

2nd paragraph: **Knights of the Askin Round Table:**
Sir Robert Askin, Liberal Premier of NSW
1965-75, received a knighthood along with
several developers known as 'Askin's Knights'.

Australian of the Year

1st paragraph: **Lucky Country:** popular idiom for Australia
derived from the ironic title of Donald Horne's
book (1964), a critique of Australian society.

Poor Henry Lawson

1st paragraph: **Henry Lawson:** Australia's best known
writer of bush stories (1867-1922).

A Noble Pair

4th paragraph: **cess:** luck (Irish).
Grazier: refers to Malcolm Fraser, Liberal
Prime Minister of Australia 1975-83 and an
established rural landowner.

7th paragraph: **H. V. Evatt:** Australia's chief representative
at the newly formed United Nations
Organization and first president of the
General Assembly 1948-49.

Citizens For Democracy

10th paragraph: **Macbeth:** refers to Sir John Kerr, Governor-
General of Australia 1974-77, who dismissed
the Whitlam Labor Government on 11
November 1975.
Yarralumla: Governor-General's residence in
Canberra.

caretaker: refers to Malcolm Fraser, appointed caretaker Prime Minister of Australia following the sacking of the Whitlam Labor Government.

13th paragraph: **Lord De L'Isle:** William Philip Sidney, British-born Governor-General of Australia 1961-65.

The Reading Sickness
1st paragraph: **Mrs Wran:** wife of Neville Wran, Labor Premier of NSW.

Truth and Fiction
4th paragraph: **Professor Kramer:** Dame Leonie Kramer, Professor of Australian Literature, University of Sydney.

State of the Colony
6th paragraph: **Governor-General:** Sir Zelman Cowan 1977-82.

8th paragraph: **Smith Family:** a charitable institution renowned for its work among the poor and homeless.

14th paragraph: **Governor-General:** Sir John Kerr 1974-77.

Jack Mundey and the BLF
3rd paragraph: **commo:** communist.

A Letter to Humanity
4th paragraph: **Harold Holt:** Liberal Prime Minister of Australia 1966-67.

A New Constitution
6th paragraph: **Sir Neddy:** refers to artist Sir Sidney Nolan who painted a series based on Australia's bushranger hero Ned Kelly.

Hiroshima Day
20th paragraph: **New Zealander:** David Lange, Labour Prime Minister of New Zealand.

Monsterail
1st paragraph: **Brereton:** Laurie Brereton, then NSW Labor Minister for Public Works and Ports.
Sir Peter Abeles: very powerful businessman and managing director of Thomas Nationwide Transport (TNT) which runs Sydney's monorail.
Hooker/Harrah: business consortium which tended for the Darling Harbour casino licence.

Imagining the Real
11th paragraph: **Maralinga:** desert site in South Australia of secret British nuclear bomb tests in the 1950s.

The Bicentenary
8th paragraph: **Packer:** Kerry Packer, heir to media empire, multi-millionaire businessman, and punter.
Bondie: Alan Bond, West Australian self-made multi-millionaire entrepreneur and speculator.
Blowie: blowfly.

9th paragraph: **cardies:** cardigans.

A Sense of Integrity
21st paragraph: **BILL:** Bill Hayden, Deputy Prime Minister (ALP), about to leave Parliament and become Governor-General of Australia.

Brizzy: Brisbane.

FOR THE BEST IN PAPERBACKS, LOOK FOR THE 🐧

In every corner of the world, on every subject under the sun, Penguin represents quality and variety – the very best in publishing today.

For complete information about books available from Penguin – including Puffins, Penguin Classics and Arkana – and how to order them, write to us at the appropriate address below. Please note that for copyright reasons the selection of books varies from country to country.

In the United Kingdom: Please write to *Dept JC, Penguin Books Ltd, FREEPOST, West Drayton, Middlesex, UB7 0BR.*

If you have any difficulty in obtaining a title, please send your order with the correct money, plus ten per cent for postage and packaging, to *PO Box No 11, West Drayton, Middlesex*

In the United States: Please write to *Dept BA, Penguin, 299 Murray Hill Parkway, East Rutherford, New Jersey 07073*

In Canada: Please write to *Penguin Books Canada Ltd, 2801 John Street, Markham, Ontario L3R 1B4*

In Australia: Please write to the *Marketing Department, Penguin Books Australia Ltd, P.O. Box 257, Ringwood, Victoria 3134*

In New Zealand: Please write to the *Marketing Department, Penguin Books (NZ) Ltd, Private Bag, Takapuna, Auckland 9*

In India: Please write to *Penguin Overseas Ltd, 706 Eros Apartments, 56 Nehru Place, New Delhi, 110019*

In the Netherlands: Please write to *Penguin Books Netherlands B.V., Postbus 3507, NL–1001 AH, Amsterdam*

In West Germany: Please write to *Penguin Books Ltd, Friedrichstrasse 10–12, D–6000 Frankfurt/Main 1*

In Spain: Please write to *Alhambra Longman S.A., Fernandez de la Hoz 9, E–28010 Madrid*

In Italy: Please write to *Penguin Italia s.r.l., Via Como 4, I-20096 Pioltello (Milano)*

In France: Please write to *Penguin France S.A., 17 rue Lejeune, F-31000 Toulouse*

In Japan: Please write to *Longman Penguin Japan Co Ltd, Yamaguchi Building, 2–12–9 Kanda Jimbocho, Chiyoda-Ku, Tokyo 101*

A SELECTION OF FICTION AND NON-FICTION

Perfume Patrick Süskind

It was after his first murder that Grenouille knew he was a genius. He was to become the greatest perfumer of all time, for he possessed the power to distil the very essence of love itself. 'Witty, stylish and ferociously absorbing' – *Observer*

A Confederacy of Dunces John Kennedy Toole

In this Pulitzer Prize-winning novel, in the bulky figure of Ignatius J. Reilly, an immortal comic character is born. 'I succumbed, stunned and seduced ... a masterwork of comedy' – *The New York Times*

In the Land of Oz Howard Jacobson

'The most successful attempt I know to grip the great dreaming Australian enigma by the throat and make it gargle' – *Evening Standard*. 'Sharp characterization, crunching dialogue and self-parody ... a sharp, skilful and brilliantly funny book' – *Literary Review*

The World as I Found It Bruce Duffy

From Freud's Vienna to Russell's Cambridge, from World War I to the Bloomsbury Set, this extraordinary work – novel, philosophical history and imaginative biography – charts the turbulent career of the philosopher Ludwig Wittgenstein and his stormy relationships with G. E. Moore and Bertrand Russell. 'Racy, accessible and pleasurable' – *The Times*

The Memory of War and Children in Exile: Poems 1968–83 James Fenton

'James Fenton is a poet I find myself again and again wanting to praise' – *Listener*. 'His assemblages bring with them tragedy, comedy, love of the world's variety, and the sadness of its moral blight' – *Observer*

The Bloody Chamber Angela Carter

In tales that glitter and haunt – strange nuggets from a writer whose wayward pen spills forth stylish, erotic, nightmarish jewels of prose – the old fairy stories live and breathe again, subtly altered, subtly changed.

FOR THE BEST IN PAPERBACKS, LOOK FOR THE 🐧

A SELECTION OF FICTION AND NON-FICTION

The Great Indian Novel   Shashi Tharoor

In a dazzling marriage of Hindu myth and modern history, Sashi Tharoor reinvents India. 'Vastly enjoyable ... a *tour de force* of considerable brilliance ... *The Great Indian Novel* never fails to hold our attention' – *The Times Literary Supplement*

The Purple Decades   Tom Wolfe

From Surfers to Moonies, from *The Electric Kool-Aid Acid Test* to *The Right Stuff*, a technicolour retrospective from the foremost chronicler of the gaudiest period in American history.

Still Life   A. S. Byatt

Frederica Potter, 'doomed to be intelligent', plunges into the university life of 1950s Cambridge greedy for knowledge, sex and love. In Yorkshire her sister Stephanie has abandoned academe for the cosy frustration of the family. 'Affords enormous and continuous pleasure' – Anita Brookner

The Moronic Inferno   Martin Amis

'Really good reading and sharp, crackling writing. Amis has a beguiling mixture of confidence and courtesy, and most of his literary judgments – often twinned with interviews – seem sturdy, even when caustic, without being bitchy for the hell of it' – *Guardian*

The Silence in the Garden   William Trevor

'Subtle, intricate and beautiful ... Mr Trevor's compassion for his characters ... makes this novel of decline and melancholy decay an affirmation of the goodness and rich variety of life ... No-one interested in what fiction can do to illuminate and enrich life should fail to read this book' – Allan Massie

The Guide   R. K. Narayan

Raju, recently released from prison, used to be India's most corrupt tourist guide. Then a peasant mistakes him for a holy man – and gradually he begins to play the part. He succeeds so well that God himself intervenes to put his new holiness to the test.

FOR THE BEST IN PAPERBACKS, LOOK FOR THE

A SELECTION OF FICTION AND NON-FICTION

The Dictionary of the Khazars Milorad Pavić

'Borges and Nabokov, Singer and Calvino, Eco's *The Name of the Rose* – Pavić's novel conjures up images (dreams?) of some of our century's most enthralling imaginative literature … I would say that in its teasing way it is a masterpiece' – *Sunday Times*

Travels in the Drifting Dawn Kenneth White

Beginning in the underground London of the sixties and the Glasgow of the same period, where he was a 'non-secret agent' for William Burroughs' and Alex Trocchi's Project Sigma, the wanderings of Kenneth White have carried him from Ireland to North Africa to the very edges of western culture.

My Father's Moon Elizabeth Jolley

Vera Wright was a boarding-school girl, then a nurse in wartime England, the era of air-raids, rationing and tangos on the gramophone, when all the girls waited for letters, and some of them waited for love.

Einstein's Monsters Martin Amis

'This collection of five stories and an introductory essay … announces an obsession with nuclear weapons; it also announces a new tonality in Amis's writing' – John Lanchester in the *London Review of Books*

In the Heart of the Country J. M. Coetzee

In a web of reciprocal oppression in colonial South Africa, a white sheep farmer makes a bid for salvation in the arms of a black concubine, while his embittered daughter dreams of and executes a bloody revenge. Or does she?

Baumgartner's Bombay Anita Desai

'Hugo Baumgartner, the central character in Anita Desai's dazzling new novel, is a wandering Jew all his life … Too dark for Hitler's society, he is too fair for India; he remains a *firanghi*, a foreigner wherever he goes' – *Daily Telegraph*. 'The achievement of a superior writer' – *Literary Review*

Cal   Bernard Mac Laverty

Springing out of the fear and violence of Ulster, *Cal* is a haunting love story from a land where tenderness and innocence can only flicker briefly in the dark. 'Mac Laverty describes the sad, straitened, passionate lives of his characters with tremendously moving skill' – *Spectator*

The Rebel Angels   Robertson Davies

A glittering extravaganza of wit, scatology, saturnalia, mysticism and erudite vaudeville. 'The kind of writer who makes you want to nag your friends until they read him so that they can share the pleasure' – *Observer*

Stars of the New Curfew   Ben Okri

'Anarchical energy with authoritative poise ... an electrifying collection' – Graham Swift. 'Okri's work is obsessive and compelling, spangled with a sense of exotic magic and haunted by shadows ... reality re-dreamt with great conviction' – *Time Out*

The Magic Lantern   Ingmar Bergman

'A kaleidoscope of memories intercut as in a film, sharply written and trimmed to the bone' – *Sunday Times*. 'The autobiography is exactly like the films: beautiful and repulsive; truthful and phoney; constantly startling' – *Sunday Telegraph*. 'Unique, reticent, revealing' – Lindsay Anderson

The Horn   John Clellon Holmes

Edgar Pool is slave to nothing, not even the genius inside him. He lives no life but jazz, no days but nights wrestling swing out of sordidness in the crowded clubs of New York. And out of obsession with the sound of his tenor sax the legend of bop is born... 'The people ... are real, the music is thrilling, and the writing is powerful' – *Chicago Tribune*

The News from Ireland   William Trevor

'An ability to enchant as much as chill has made Trevor unquestionably one of our greatest short-story writers' – *The Times*. 'A masterly collection' – *Daily Telegraph*

The Twyborn Affair

Eddie Twyborn is bisexual and beautiful, the son of a Judge and a drunken mother. With this androgynous hero – Eudoxia/Eddie/Eadith Twyborn – and through his search for identity, for self-affirmation and love in its many forms, Patrick White takes us on a journey into the ambiguous landscapes, sexual, psychological and spiritual, of the human condition.

Flaws in the Glass
A Self-Portrait

With force, candour and emotion, Patrick White writes of his youth in Australia, his English boarding school, his life at Cambridge and trips to Germany, London during the Blitz, RAF wartime intelligence in the Middle East and his first meeting with the man who was to become the central focus of his life.

The Living and the Dead

Set in London in the thirties, *The Living and the Dead* is concerned with the brother and sister, Elyot and Eden Standish. But beneath and behind the personal drama of their lives an entire civilization crumbles and heads for war.

and:

The Eye of the Storm

The Tree of Man

This great novel could fittingly claim to stand as the Australian Book of Genesis. A young man, at the turn of the century, takes a wife and carves out a home in the wilderness near one of the growing cities of Australia. Stan Parker becomes a small farmer: he accepts life as he finds it. To him Amy bears children and time brings a procession of ordinary events – achievements, disappointments, sorrows, dramas, dreams. There is the daily intercourse with neighbours of their kind and at the end death walks in the garden.

Voss

The plot of this novel is of epic simplicity: in 1845 Voss sets out with a small band to cross the Australian continent for the first time. The tragic story of their terrible journey and its inevitable end is told with imaginative understanding. The figure of Voss takes on superhuman proportions, until he appears to those around him as both deliverer and destroyer. His relationship with Laura Trevelyan is the central personal theme of the story. The true record of Ludwig Leichardt, who died in the Australian desert in 1848, suggested *Voss* to the author.

Riders in the Chariot

In *The Tree of Man* Patrick White re-created the Garden of Eden in Australia: *Riders in the Chariot*, his story of four outcast mystics, powerfully re-enacts the story of the crucifixion in a like setting. 'A book which really defies review: for its analysable qualities are overwhelmed by those imponderables which make a work 'great' in the untouchable sense. It must be read because, like Everest, 'it is there' – Jeremy Brooks in the *Guardian*

The Solid Mandala

This is the story of two people living one life. Arthur and Waldo Brown were born twins and destined never to grow away from each other. They spent their childhood together. Their youth together. Middle-age together. Retirement together. They even shared the same girl. They shared everything – except their views. Waldo, with his intelligence, saw everything and understood little. Arthur was the fool who didn't bother to look. He understood.

A Fringe of Leaves

With *A Fringe of Leaves* Patrick White has richly justified his Nobel Prize. Set in Australia in the 1840s, this novel combines dramatic action with a finely distilled moral vision. It is a masterpiece. Returning home to England from Van Diemen's Land, the *Bristol Maid* is shipwrecked on the Queensland coast and Mrs Roxburgh is taken prisoner by a tribe of aborigines, along with the rest of the passengers and crew. In the course of her escape, she is torn by conflicting loyalties – to her dead husband, to her rescuer, to her own and her adoptive class.

The Cockatoos

These six short novels and stories achieve the majesty and power of the best of Patrick White's great novels. They probe beneath the confused and meretricious surface, exposing the true nature of things with chiselled, polished images. 'To read Patrick White . . . is to touch a source of power, to move through areas made new and fresh, to see men and women with a sharpened gaze' – Elizabeth Berridge in the *Daily Telegraph*

BY THE SAME AUTHOR

The Vivisector

Hurtle Duffield is incapable of loving anything except what he paints. The men and women who court him during his long life are, above all, the victims of his art. He is the vivisector, dissecting their weaknesses with cruel precision: his sister's deformity, a grocer's moonlight indiscretion and the passionate illusions of his mistress Hero Pavloussi. Only the ego-centric adolescent he sees as his spiritual child elicits from him a deeper, more treacherous emotion.

The Burnt Ones

Eleven stories to which Patrick White brings his immense understanding of the urges which lie just beneath the façade of ordinary human relation-ships, especially those between men and women . . .

The Aunt's Story

Theodora Goodman is both mad and exceptionally realistic, even if her created lives were interchangeable. Tracing her uncompromisingly inde-pendent career from the dusty reality of Australia to the whirling mad-house of Europe before the Second World War, this book has the imaginative daring of *Voss* and the deep-flowing sympathy of *The Tree of Man*. *The Aunt's Story* finally comes to an end calmly – although across the borders of sanity – in that most practical of countries, the United States of America.